Learning to Succeed

a new framework for post-16 learning

Presented to Parliament by
the Secretary of State for Education and Employment
by Command of Her Majesty

June 1999

Cm 4392

£9.70

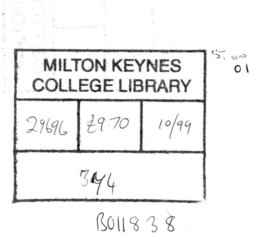

Foreword by the Secretary of State

In the Green Paper *The Learning Age* we set out our vision of how lifelong learning could enable everyone to fulfil their potential and cope with the challenge of rapid economic and social change. Lifelong learning can enable people to play a full part in developing their talent, the potential of their family, and the capacity of the community in which they live and work. It can and must nurture a love for learning. This will ensure the means by which our economy can make a successful transition from the industries and services of the past, to the knowledge and information economy of the future. It also contributes to sustaining a civilised and cohesive society, in which people develop as active citizens and in which generational disadvantage can be overcome.

The skill needs of the future will be different from those of today and it is clear that we will not keep pace with the modern economies of our competitors, if we are unable to match today's skills with the challenge of the developing information and communication age of tomorrow. As labour markets change, we must develop a new approach to skills, and to enabling people, and businesses, to succeed.

The challenge is urgent. That is why the Government has given priority to education with more than £19 billion of extra resources over three years. This priority has been widely supported and the vision of *The Learning Age* has been welcomed. But many of those who commented recommended a bold programme of change in national and local arrangements. They confirmed our view that current arrangements provided an insufficient focus on quality, failed to give men and women the support they need, and were too provider driven. Above all, there was an acknowledgement of the inconsistency and contradictions in present funding and delivery mechanisms. There was, therefore, widespread support for fundamental change, and in particular for the creation of a single body to oversee national strategies for post-16 learning, the funding to provide the focus needed, and the emphasis on quality to lever up standards.

In March this year, I announced a wide-ranging consultation about the structures for education and training for people over the age of 16, other than higher education. I undertook to publish proposals in the summer for a new framework. This White Paper sets out our proposals and invites comment on a number of issues.

We propose to establish a national Learning and Skills Council to replace the Further Education Funding Council and the Training and Enterprise Councils. The new Council will work alongside a new organisation responsible for advice and support to young people and will be complemented by an independent, rigorous and effective inspection regime. It will also forge important links with the Ufl and other key partners at a national and local level. The Council will operate through local arms that will be responsible for co-ordinating area plans building on the work of the local Learning Partnerships. The Learning and Skills Council will be responsible for the planning of around £5 billion of public money and over 5 million learners.

We will strengthen the role of business, local authorities, providers and the individual users of service, in driving the direction of the new system, through their continuing involvement in local Learning Partnerships. In addition, we will ensure that their contribution to the work of the local arms of the Learning and Skills Council, ensures the necessary focus on change outlined in this paper.

The Learning Partnerships will remain key forums to bring stakeholders together in the endeavour to improve access and opportunity. The task will be to drive up the quality of what is on offer, to ensure co-ordination and to avoid both waste and duplication. This will be crucial to matching the learning which is available, to the skills and development needs of both people and businesses in the locality.

These new arrangements will create a framework based on partnership and co-operation between individuals, businesses and communities, as well as institutions. We seek to ensure that better advice and guidance raises standards and participation among young and old alike, that individuals can make the best of their talent and potential and employers have a competitive edge in the global economy.

The new arrangements will encourage coherence, quality and success in meeting targets. This will also stimulate a spirit of self-help, which enriched the lives and raised the aspirations of those who pioneered the movement for full-time education and the drive for access to learning for all. We must place the learner at the heart of the new system.

I recognise that these proposals will involve change for many of the organisations and providers involved in delivering post-16 education, and the people who work for them. I therefore want to move forward with national and local partners to ensure that during this period of transition we continue to deliver the improvements in performance, in meeting targets, and in opening access, which we have already begun. We shall do so in a new framework based on partnership, co-operation and collaboration.

Employers and trade unionists, together with representatives of local authorities, voluntary organisations and the wider community, have already made a substantial contribution as members of Training and Enterprise Council boards, in the development of organisations such as learning cities, in the governing bodies of colleges, and as members of the Further Education Funding Council and its Regional Committees.

I would like to thank everyone for the contribution they have made, and welcome their further participation in our new structure. I am determined that we build on the best features of what we have at present, whilst seeking to remove the contradictions, conflict and incoherence which currently exists.

The task ahead is to modernise the framework for post-16 education and to raise quality. This White Paper sets out our policies to achieve the step change in performance which is needed to meet the challenge ahead. I invite all those involved to work with us, to make this the basis for substantive and lasting change and improvement, in the years ahead.

Contents

Executive Summary

Our Vision for the new Millennium (Chapter 1)

Our vision is to build a new culture of learning which will underpin national competitiveness and personal prosperity, encourage creativity and innovation and help build a cohesive society. The principles which underpin our vision are those we first set out in our green paper *The Learning Age*. They were:

- investing in learning to benefit everyone;
- lifting barriers to learning;
- putting people first;
- sharing responsibility with employers, employees and the community;
- achieving world class standards and value for money; and
- working together as the key to success.

The National Learning Targets will underpin this commitment. To achieve them, we require significant improvements in participation and attainment beyond, as much as below age 16.

Why change is necessary (Chapter 2)

Whilst significant progress has already been made, we are still a long way from achieving our vision of a learning society. Too many people are excluded from the benefits that learning can bring. Aspirations and staying on rates remain too low. The system fails a significant section of the community, often the most vulnerable. People with low skills and poor qualifications are locked in a cycle of disadvantage. We must also make education and training more relevant and accessible to both individuals and employers. And people need better advice and support and more flexible ways of learning. There are also too many providers where quality is not up to scratch and where success rates are therefore very poor.

We have already begun to tackle these problems, but we cannot achieve our vision if we ignore the fundamental weaknesses in the current systems. Mechanisms for planning and funding are complex, inconsistent and confusing. Too many administrative layers means too little money reaches learners and employers. There is insufficient focus on skill needs and a lack of innovation. In addition, the inspection system does not deliver the consistent and co-ordinated approaches necessary to drive forward higher standards and clear accountability.

In drawing up proposals for change, we have been guided by the following principles:

- change should promote excellence and participation;
- employers should have a substantial stake in shaping post-16 education and training;
- systems must be learner driven and responsive to the needs of individuals, businesses and their communities;
- equal access to education, training and skills opportunities should be a priority, with equal opportunity in the mainstream of provision;
- people should have access to support in the form of good advice and guidance and, where appropriate, financial help; and
- accountability, efficiency and probity should be promoted at every level.

The Learning and Skills Council (Chapter 3)

We propose to establish a Learning and Skills Council for England to drive forward improvements in standards and bring greater coherence and responsiveness. The Council will deliver all post-16 education and training (excluding HE) and assume responsibility for:

- funding colleges from the Further Education Funding Council for England;

- advising the Government on the National Learning Targets from the National Advisory Council for Education and Training Targets (NACETT);

- funding Modern Apprenticeships, National Traineeships and other government funded training and workforce development from Training and Enterprise Councils (TECs)[1];

- developing, in partnership with local education authorities (LEAs), arrangements for adult and community learning;

- providing information, advice and guidance to adults; and

- working with the pre-16 education sector to ensure coherence across all 14-19 education.

We propose to establish the new Learning and Skills Council from April 2001. Key features will be:

- a system driven by the needs of the learner including the significant involvement of employers. The majority of the Council's members will be users of learning (employers, individuals, local authorities and community representatives);

- the Council will be advised by two Committees of the Council: one with direct responsibility for young people; the other with responsibility for adult learners. The Committees will advise the Council and assess the needs of their respective groups in the context of present and future labour market skills, and advise on action and strategies;

- the Council will work through a network of up to 50 local Learning and Skills Councils, which will plan and co-ordinate provision locally and establish clear lines of accountability to the communities they serve. These local Learning and Skills Councils will be arms of the national Council but with sufficient local flexibility and autonomy to allow them to match provision to local needs and meet skill shortages. Their work will be overseen by Boards who - as with the national Council - will have a majority of members who can represent users of learning locally;

- local Learning Partnerships will be at the heart of these new arrangements. This will ensure that the system is fully responsive to local partners and community needs. We propose a new role for them in drawing up arrangements for consultative mechanisms through which the voice of individual learners can be heard and fed back to improve the quality of provision; and

- improved accountability, efficiency and probity.

The Learning and Skills Council will promote equality of opportunity in all it does.

[1] The references in this paper to TECs cover English TECs only and also cover Chambers of Commerce, Training and Enterprise (CCTEs).

A Framework for Success Beyond 16 (Chapter 4)

We propose to build a new system of planning and funding post-16 education and training that will overcome the complexity of the existing system and cut unnecessary layers of bureaucracy. The new system will simplify arrangements and make it easier for money to get to the learner. It will promote flexibility and customer focused learning, drawing on the experience of the Ufl. It will also support equality of opportunity and meet the needs of people who face particular disadvantages in the labour market.

Within these arrangements, it will be essential that the local Learning and Skills Councils have local flexibility and autonomy in significant areas of their work. By agreement with the national Council, they will have the scope to vary the national funding tariff, for example, in relation to particular local needs and skill shortages. They will also manage local budgets for quality improvement, building capacity in providers, adult and community learning, education business partnerships, Investors in People and other areas where local flexibility is important.

Regional Development Agencies (RDAs) will have a key role in the planning arrangements for learning and skills, with a strong link between the RDAs and the Learning and Skills Council both at national and local level. Local Councils' plans will reflect the needs and priorities of the region set out in the RDA's regional strategy; and RDAs will work with local Councils to assess how well regional skills needs are met.

We will be consulting on the new planning and funding system and the ways in which we can strike the right balance between national arrangements and local flexibility.

We will also establish systems to evaluate the success of the new arrangements. An essential part of the evaluation will be ensuring good quality information about outcomes and their impact at national and local level.

Improving Quality (Chapter 5)

We expect the Learning and Skills Council only to fund learning which meets its quality standards and probity requirements and to take firm action where providers are falling short of these standards. The Learning and Skills Council will be responsible for drawing up a quality improvement strategy. The Council will also reward high quality in education and training provision building on the accredited and Beacon status introduced for FE colleges.

These quality standards need to be supported by new **rigorous, independent inspection arrangements.** To improve coherence, we will bring together the inspection processes for young people learning in schools and colleges through to the age of 19. OFSTED will be responsible for the inspection of this provision. We want in addition to combine current arrangements to create a new independent Inspectorate which will assess the quality of provision for adults and of all work based training. The new Inspectorate will work closely with OFSTED to ensure a common approach to inspection.

Education and Training of Young People (Chapter 6)

Young people deserve the chance to be better qualified and to have the best possible start to their working lives. We propose to publish shortly a strategy - called *Connexions* - for making sure that far more young people continue in education and training through their teenage years until they are at least 19. Ensuring young people have the help, support and guidance that will raise their aspirations and tackle problems which stand in the way will be essential. We are introducing - progressively from September - a Learning Gateway for 16 and 17 year olds who need extra guidance and support to benefit from mainstream learning. Central to this will be the development of a network of personal advisers.

We propose to create new arrangements for providing support to young people, based on this concept of personal advisers. Its prime function will be to create a comprehensive structure for advice and support for all young people from the age of 13, improving the coherence of what is currently provided through organisations such as the Careers Service, parts of the Youth Service and a range of other specialist agencies. The new service will present a step change in the way this support is provided to young people, ensuring a smooth transition from compulsory schooling to post-16 learning. The new service will need an innovative, effective and consistent means of local delivery, building on best current practice. It will be organised on the same geographical areas as the local Learning and Skills Councils.

Supporting Adult Learners (Chapter 7)

The Learning and Skills Council will work with others to champion lifelong learning for all. The Council will have a clear role to play in driving up demand for learning so as to complement the impact of individual learning accounts and the Ufl and support the work of NIACE, the Campaign for Learning and broadcasters in promoting learning throughout life. The Learning and Skills Council will work closely with the Ufl to improve the overall coherence and responsiveness of education and training provision for adults and embed lifelong learning in people's daily lives. It will have a responsibility for funding high quality information, advice and guidance for adults, working closely with the Ufl's Learning Direct national helpline and a national duty to secure adult and community learning provision, to which local authorities will have the duty to contribute.

We also propose a more integrated service for unemployed people, by transferring responsibility for work based learning for adults from TECs to the Employment Service from April 2001, so that it becomes part of a coherent set of programmes, alongside the New Deals and the new ONE service for benefit claimants.

Encouraging Learning Businesses (Chapter 8)

Businesses need a well motivated and skilled workforce to compete in global markets. Successful employers are those who realise that people are their most important asset - and act on that by investing in their skills and development. The proposals for a Learning and Skills Council at national and local level will give employers unprecedented influence over the education system and promote a better match between demand and supply for skills.

At national level the Learning and Skills Council will build better sources of labour market and skills information, drawing in up to date information on sectoral trends from the National Training Organisations, as a basis for the preparation and publication of a strategy for skills and workforce development and an annual skills assessment for the nation. They will develop new initiatives to improve the opportunities that individuals in the workplace have to acquire skills, drawing on the experience of UfI and trade union initiatives such as *Bargaining for Skills*. The network of local councils will identify and disseminate best practice in work based training, drawing on initiatives such as the *People Skills Scoreboard*.

At local level, Learning and Skills Councils will provide a wide range of practical help to individual businesses, for example support in developing effective training plans, advice and support for Investors in People, support for critical skills development and help with recruitment for Modern Apprenticeships and National Traineeships. They will also develop new approaches to collaborative working between employers, for example setting up networks of employers in a particular sector to identify key skill needs for the sector and work with colleges and providers to establish effective supply chain responses and 'preferred supplier arrangements'. Local Learning and Skills Councils will also encourage businesses to set up 'employee development' schemes, linking them to individual learning accounts to stimulate demand for learning from individuals.

Local Learning and Skills Councils' plans will be developed in conjunction with the new Small Business Service, for example by arranging for the Small Business Service to provide a seamless service to small and medium sized businesses and to integrate skills development with enterprise and business competitiveness.

Transitional arrangements (Chapter 9)

We recognise that the next two years will be a challenging period for all involved in post-16 learning. Work will need to continue in order to achieve the ambitious targets we have set to increase participation, attainment and the quality of services we offer to young people and adults. Making the necessary changes in structures must not hinder that crucial task. We are therefore publishing at the same time as this White Paper the first draft of a transition plan. This plan will be the basis for detailed discussions with each organisation involved in our proposals.

Next steps

These proposals have benefited from the wide range of responses to our invitation to contribute to our review of post-16 provision. This White Paper sets out proposals for major change. We have invited comments on some specific issues. On others, we have explained that we will publish further discussion papers over the next few months. If we are to ensure that the very significant public investment we make in post-16 learning serves people better, we want to know what you think of our proposals and involve you in developing the solutions.

How to respond

The issues for consultation are highlighted in the text and summarised in Chapter 10 - which also sets out how to respond. Contributions and comments on these issues are invited by 15 October 1999.

Position in Scotland, Wales and Northern Ireland

The arrangements apply to England only. The implications for post-16 learning in Scotland, Wales and Northern Ireland are described in Appendix 1.

CHAPTER 1

A vision for the new millennium

The challenge

1.1   The challenge we face to equip individuals, employers and the country to meet the demands of the 21st century is immense and immediate. In the information and knowledge based economy, investment in human capital - in the intellect and creativity of people - is replacing past patterns of investment in plant, machinery and physical labour. To continue to compete, we must equip ourselves for this new world with new and better skills. We must improve levels of knowledge and understanding and develop the adaptability to respond to change.

1.2   For our companies to succeed on the world stage, they will need to be learning, innovative businesses. The notion of "leaving education at 16" must pass into history. For our people to prosper, they will need access to learning throughout their working lives so as to keep their qualifications up to date and, where necessary, to train for new or changing jobs. To do this, we will need to:

- increase our skill levels to match those of our competitors;

- achieve a step change in the aspirations of individuals and improve the quality and range of opportunities for learning available to them;

- tackle social exclusion at its roots within the education system both before and beyond the school leaving age; and

- focus on the employability of the labour force as well as on employment.

1.3   The existing framework for post-16 education and training does not support these goals. Too many people drop out at 16. Too little support and guidance is offered to young people as they face the most critical career decisions of their lives. The range and quality of opportunities available to those who stay on - or proceed to work based training - are too often insufficient. For adults, there remain barriers to returning to education and training and similar problems of insufficient information, advice and opportunity. We have started to tackle these problems and there are examples of imaginative responses to the challenge by employers, further education and the TEC system. But much more remains to be done.

The scale of the challenge

1.4   Productivity in the UK is lower than in other major economies. The Gross Domestic Product per worker in the UK lags behind the US by almost 40% and behind France and Germany by around 20%. The hallmark of our inadequate performance is the lower skill levels at intermediate and technician levels of our workforce. The 1996 Skills Audit showed that the UK performs well against some of our competitors in qualifications at level 4 (first degree or equivalent) and above, but poorly at the intermediate and technician levels.

1.5 Although there has been an improvement in the UK's position since the Skills Audit, this has generally also been the case in other countries. For example, in 1998 the proportion of adults in the UK with qualifications at technician level and above was still only half that of Germany, mainly because of the large number of Germans who have gone through apprenticeship training. Other evidence suggests that the proportion of UK adults with qualifications at intermediate level and above is well below that of France.

1.6 There are too many people with few, if any, qualifications and too many with low skills. Lack of skills reduces people's chances of well-paid and steady employment. Those without qualifications earn 30% less than average earnings. The earnings of people with degrees are double those of people with no qualifications. The unemployment rate of those with no qualifications is more than three times that of graduates. Without urgent action to tackle these problems, the risks of social exclusion will grow as sophistication in information and other new technologies increases. Society will continue to be divided between the information rich and the information poor.

Our vision

1.7 Our vision of the Learning Age is to build a new culture of learning and aspiration which will underpin national competitiveness and personal prosperity, encourage creativity and innovation and help build a more cohesive society. We want everyone to benefit from the opportunities that learning brings both in personal growth and the enrichment of communities.

1.8 This vision takes account of the sea changes that have taken place in the economy, particularly the impact of information and communication technology in the workplace. Employers rightly put a premium on adaptability and the capacity to learn new skills. The strengths of the past apprenticeship and craft system need to be replicated in a new age, while meeting the challenge of a rapidly changing competitive economy. In the digital age, learning must take place 'on-site' in small and medium sized companies as well as in large businesses.

Principles

1.9 The principles that underpin our vision are those we first set out in *The Learning Age*.

They were:

- investing in learning to benefit everyone;
- lifting barriers to learning;
- putting people first;
- sharing responsibility with employers, employees and the community;
- achieving world class standards and value for money; and
- working together as the key to success.

We believe that these principles should guide and inform the development of a new framework of post-16 learning for the 21st century.

Participation and standards

1.10 The National Learning Targets - see below - underpin our commitment to widen and increase participation in learning and raise the attainment levels of people entering education and training.

National Learning Targets	current	2002 target
19 year olds with Level 2	74%	85%
21 year olds with Level 3	52%	60%
Adults with Level 3	45%	50%
Adults with Level 4	26%	28%
7% reduction in non learners		
Medium sized or large organisations recognised as Investors in People	30%	45%
Small organisations recognised as Investors in People	2,800	10,000

1.11 The Government recognises that the achievement of these targets will require a substantial improvement in participation and achievement at every level. The Government has already acted to improve performance towards these targets through a programme of investment in further education and training and a range of other steps, e.g. the UFI and individual learning accounts - set out in our Green Paper *The Learning Age*. This work builds on the improvements in school standards being taken forward nationwide. We must ensure that post-16 learning is ready for the improvement in the qualifications, aptitudes and aspirations of 16 year olds which is taking place year by year. It must be able to take these young people onwards. We must also ensure that learning providers are responsive to the needs of adults.

1.12 We are also already taking action to improve the skills of the workforce. A key feature of our Welfare to Work programme is to ensure that people develop the skills they need to be effective in the labour market. Almost 300,000 young people have joined New Deal - a programme with employability at its heart. Modern Apprenticeships are raising the standard of work based training and ensuring a better supply of vocational skills. Our further education system is responding to changing needs. Our higher education system is second to none in quality. Participation in higher education is up to one in three young people.

A new partnership

1.13 A key element of the proposed new arrangements will be a shared responsibility in the new century for achieving a lifelong learning culture between the Government, individuals, employers, providers and communities. Each must accept the challenges of promoting and participating in learning and working towards common goals. All will benefit from this investment of time, energy and resources. Learning will make a reality of self-reliance, self-confidence, employability and adaptability both for business and individuals and the communities in which they live. Together we will need to ensure that the new arrangements meet the skills needs of localities, regions and the nation for the years ahead.

1.14 The Government is committed to investing in the economic, social and institutional framework. We will provide incentives and encouragement to all partners, ensuring that worthwhile opportunities are available, supported and funded which are of benefit to individuals, the economy and communities. We will generate a structure of learning and qualifications which complements and extends the training provided by employers. We will provide a lead in promoting the development of new opportunities to meet future skills needs.

1.15 The Government's role in the new arrangements will be to steer the system, to set the necessary economic, social and institutional framework. We will:

- provide support, incentives and encouragement;
- ensure opportunities are available, accessible and funded;
- complement the training provided by employers;
- focus on individuals, employers and communities; and
- ensure the development of new opportunities to meet future skill needs.

1.16 The achievement of our vision will depend on each partner taking an active role. In setting the new framework, we will look to:

- individuals to take responsibility for their own future assisted by intensive advice and support, to seek opportunities to improve their knowledge, understanding and skills; and to make their own investment in personal success;
- employers to take responsibility for improving the skills of their workforce; and to offer their knowledge and support to local Learning Partnerships and to the new Learning and Skills Council;
- communities and their representatives, particularly local education authorities, to support and extend adult and community learning, and to continue to offer their distinctive contribution to local Learning Partnerships and to our new national and local arrangements; and
- providers to be accountable for providing responsive, high quality and effective education and training whether purchased with public or private funds.

1.17 The local Learning Partnerships will have a central role in working with providers to assist them to address local skills needs and helping both to assess and respond to local demand. The local Learning and Skills Councils will take a strategic view of the provision made locally, and have discretionary funding available to support local priorities or to stimulate local demand. The national Learning and Skills Council's responsibility will be to drive the system forward within the framework set by Government and to take responsibility for the achievement of the National Learning Targets.

Purpose of White Paper

1.18 This White Paper explains how the Government plans to realise its vision through a new partnership. The following chapters set out in detail how we aim to drive up standards and performance by removing the structural barriers within the current system. Standing still is not an option. The world has changed and the current systems and structures are real obstacles to success. Our aims can only be achieved through new arrangements at national and local level which build on the strengths, and eliminate the weaknesses, of the present arrangements.

1.19 We set out in detail throughout this paper the case for change, the new arrangements which we will put in place and how they will affect both learners of all ages and business. We look forward to working with all our partners to modernise performance and standards of learning.

CHAPTER 2

Why change is necessary

Current system - strengths and weaknesses

2.1 We can only deliver our vision by driving up standards and performance in all areas of post-16 learning provision. Good progress has been made in a number of areas under the current structure:

• the further education sector has delivered a 15% rise in the number of funded full-time equivalent students and a 13% efficiency gain in the last four years;

• TECs have built up the number of Modern Apprentices to over 100,000 in the last four years and helped over 12,000 employers to become recognised as Investors in People since 1994;

• the percentage of 17 year olds in maintained school sixth forms achieving at least two GCE A level passes has increased from 30% to 69% over a ten year period; and

• there has been a rise from 84.2% at the end of 1997 to 85.6% at the end of 1998 in the proportion of 16 years old participating in education or training, reversing a gentle decline since 1994.

2.2 There are many examples of excellent progress by FE colleges and other providers in modernising the delivery of learning; and we have established a University for Industry (UfI) to become the flagship and a focus for future innovation. Generally, however, much more needs to be done to reach out and respond to the needs of learners and potential learners, and to maximise use of and access to our schools, colleges and community assets for the benefit both of individual citizens and employers. The current system is failing a significant section of the community, often the most vulnerable and disadvantaged. It is also failing to match skills to the needs of the local labour market. For some the current system is not working. The problems include:

• **low rates of learning and staying on rates at 16** - over 160,000 young people between 16 and 18 - around one in 11 of the age group - are neither in learning nor in work; a proportion which has remained virtually unchanged since 1994. Among 16 year olds, the proportion not in full-time education or work based training ranges from about 5% to about 30% across TEC areas;

• **a cycle of deprivation and disadvantage** - people with low skills and poor qualifications are the least able to respond to the challenges of the knowledge-based economy. They are more likely to be disengaged or excluded from society. And their children are likely to follow in their footsteps. This cycle of deprivation and disadvantage was graphically set out in the Social Exclusion Unit's report *Bringing Britain Together: a National Strategy for Neighbourhood Renewal*;

• **particular difficulties faced by people with special needs** - disabled people are more than twice as likely to have no formal qualifications and are only half as likely to be in employment;

• **poor levels of basic skills amongst adults** - seven million adults have severe problems with basic skills. One in five adults has a lower level of literacy than is expected of an 11 year-old. As the Moser report found, for many people, low basic skills mean serious disadvantages at work (many are unemployed) and limits on what life can offer;

- **skill shortages and recruitment difficulties for employers.** While TECs have engaged many employers in Modern Apprenticeships and Investors in People, there are still major recruitment problems in some occupations. There also remain significant 'skills gaps' between what employers need to meet their business objectives and the skills that people possess. Evidence suggests that recruitment difficulties are roughly at the same level as 1990, and they are particularly acute in small businesses and the new technology industries. Over 80% of IT companies recruiting in 1997 experienced difficulties in finding suitable staff;

- **patchy support, advice and guidance for young people** - there are many examples of schools, voluntary organisations, careers services and employers providing the help needed to ease the move to further learning at the end of compulsory education. There are also good examples of work experience programmes for those aged 15 and 16, and of curriculum-focused projects based on school-business links. But the picture is far from consistent and the volume and quality of service is not uniform; and

- **too much learning provision which is unsuited to the needs of learners.** Many learners do not want to be tied to learning in a classroom. Many adults, in particular, are looking to learn in informal self-directed and flexible ways - in the evenings, in their places of work, at weekends and in their holidays. This flexibility will be essential if we are to attract into learning those for whom traditional learning methods have formed a barrier - including women returners and those turned off learning in a classroom by poor experiences at school.

2.3 We need to raise the aspirations of individuals and remove barriers to learning. This means arrangements that deliver our commitment to providing childcare and other support facilities; making flexible teaching arrangements to encourage participation amongst people with family responsibilities; and supporting those who return to learning to ease the transition and to reduce drop out. We must make education and training more relevant both to individuals and employers. In order to make effective decisions about their choices, individuals require accurate and up to date advice about learning opportunities and future employment prospects.

2.4 We also need to address the very large differences in performance and quality within each sector which lead to inadequate standards and poor quality provision. For example:

- in maintained school sixth forms, A level performance[1] varies from an average of around 5 A level points per student to around 30 points. Sixth forms with less than 50 students do not perform as well, on average, as those with 200 students or more;

- in further education colleges, the in-year retention rate for full-time students varies from around 70% to nearly 100%; and of those who complete, the proportion achieving their qualification aim varies from around 30% to nearly 100%;

- in TEC funded training the proportion of young people who complete their training varies from around 40% to around 70%; and of those who complete, the proportion achieving a full qualification ranges from around 40% to around 75%.

[1] The definition is average points score per candidate aged 16-18 entered for two or more GCE A-levels or AS equivalent. An A grade counts 10 points, B counts 8 points etc.

Our commitment

2.5 We have given a priority to education and training. And we have already begun to tackle these problems with a £19 billion additional investment in education over three years and new policies and initiatives which will make a difference to the opportunities for people and businesses. Examples of action already begun include:

tackling social exclusion and increasing access and participation

for young people by...

- increasing flexibility in Key Stage 4 (i.e. between the ages of 14 and 16) to allow more opportunities for work-related learning for those in schools;

- measures to encourage and enable all young people to stay in learning beyond the age of 16, in particular through focusing the Careers Service on establishing a network of personal advisors and learning gateways from September 1999, to support those young people who need it;

- a new employment right for employees aged 16-17 who did not achieve good qualifications at school, to study or train for approved qualifications, with the support of their employer;

- working with the National Education Business Partnership (NEBP) to establish a quality framework for Education Business Partnerships (EBPs);

- piloting from September 1999, Education Maintenance Allowances for 16-19 year olds which will target support on young people from low income families who might otherwise be excluded;

for adults by...

- introducing pilot individual learning accounts, which next year will be developed into a national framework;

- investing £54 million over the next three years to develop and improve information, advice and guidance services for adults;

for everyone by...

- increasing the number of further education students by 700,000, and the number of higher education students by 100,000;

- establishing the Ufl which will be launched in 2000 as a distributed learning network to stimulate demand for learning in businesses and individuals, and to improve access to relevant, high quality learning opportunities;

- introducing the FE Standards Fund (£115m from 1999-2001) to help the majority of colleges to raise their performance generally; target weak colleges to allow rapid improvement; and reward excellent colleges by allowing them to spread their good practice building on the accredited Beacon Status;

- establishing local Learning Partnerships to drive forward local action on the National Targets;

enhancing employability and skills by...

- promoting the benefits of being recognised as an Investor in People to small and medium sized companies, as a basis for improving learning at work;

- establishing Regional Development Agencies (RDAs) with a broad remit which covers economic development and regeneration, and specifically includes the development and application of skills relevant to employment in their areas. RDAs will draw up regional economic strategies - and their budgets will include £39m for their work in identifying the future skills needs of employers, so they can pump prime innovative ways of meeting them;

- setting up the Skills Task Force and developing the network of National Training Organisations in 70 sectors to increase our understanding of national skill needs in the economy;

- introducing New Deal to help young and long-term unemployed people into sustained employment, with greatly enhanced opportunities for education and training; and

developing a community focus by...

- boosting opportunities for community learning with an investment of £20 million for the Adult and Community Learning Fund enhanced by the New Opportunities Fund, and investing £10.5 million in the new Union Learning Fund.

2.6 These changes will bring significant improvements. But there are fundamental weaknesses in the funding and planning systems, and in the regime for inspection and quality control which require more radical action. These are described below.

Weaknesses in the current funding and planning systems

2.7 Publicly funded education and training for those over 16 - other than those in higher education - is planned and financed through the block grant to local authorities for schools and adult education; through the Further Education Funding Council to colleges in the FE sector, universities, external institutions and other training providers; and through TECs for work based training provided by employers as well as by private, public and voluntary sector training providers. Each system works differently for the purpose of planning, funding, audit and inspection because they have evolved piecemeal, on the initiative of successive Governments and under different Government departments. The differences are hard to justify and confusing for learners and providers. Each of the three systems has its distinctive weaknesses:

- funding school sixth forms through council tax, supplemented by a block grant based on Standard Spending Assessments allows local judgements about priorities but provides too few incentives for excellence and improvement;

- the tariff-based FEFC funding regime is relatively simple and transparent and has supported a major expansion in participation in further education at relatively modest bureaucratic cost. But current tariffs were designed to meet the needs of colleges, not the skills needs of employers and individuals; and

- funding through TECs can at its best ensure that work based training is highly responsive to the needs of local employers, but the system carries a large overhead with 72 different funding and administrative systems. At its worst, the system can mean a long chain of intermediaries. This can blur lines of accountability and the extra administrative costs absorb resources which would otherwise benefit the trainee. The chart overleaf shows the length of some contracting with the existing system.

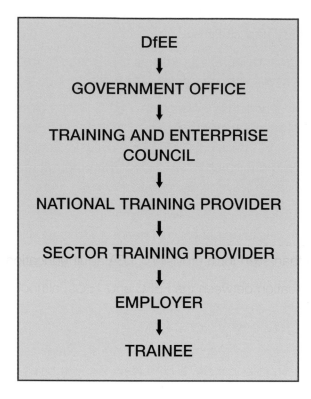

2.8   The interaction between these separate systems has resulted in a bureaucratic minefield that is confusing, difficult to negotiate and often impedes rather than encourages the learner as we can see from the following examples:

- there are insufficiently clear boundaries between the responsibility of different organisations. It is possible for the same NVQ in the same FE college to be funded (at different rates) either via the Further Education Funding Council or via a TEC, depending on whether a student is classified as full-time or part-time;

- a young person on a Modern Apprenticeship may need to have their qualification funded partly by the TEC and partly by the FEFC if they want to study for a qualification outside the mandatory part of a Modern Apprenticeship framework;

- the boundary between adult "schedule 2" courses (mainly but not exclusively leading to qualifications) which are funded by the FEFC and non-schedule 2 courses (i.e. all other adult learning), the principal responsibility for which currently rests with the local education authority (LEA), is confused and open to various interpretations;

- the complexity of the current system makes it difficult for careers advisers and teachers to help young people and their parents choose the education and training which would best meet the needs of the learner; and

- attempts to extend the curriculum for pupils aged 14-16 who would benefit from greater access to work-related learning and/or attendance at an FE college have been hindered by dislocation between the different funding systems.

Weaknesses in the inspection and quality control system

2.9 Similar types of provision have different quality assurance systems and are inspected by different agencies according to their location. For example:

- the Moser report comments that there are three different inspectorates - FEFC, TSC and OFSTED - operating in the area of adult basic skills with different frameworks and criteria. It makes recommendations for harmonising inspection approaches. A levels and GNVQs are inspected by both OFSTED and FEFC;

- schools sixth forms are inspected by OFSTED, while identical types of provision in colleges are inspected by the FEFC on a wholly different basis;

- the frequency of inspections varies. FEFC and TEC funded provision is inspected and reported on more frequently than sixth form provision. LEA adult education is hardly inspected at all;

- there has been duplication between the FEFC and TECs, although there has been recent agreement of new working arrangements to improve co-operation in relation to inspection;

- there are no shared frameworks, self-assessment arrangements, grading systems, formats for reports, or post-inspection requirements; and

- different intervention arrangements and performance indicators hinder benchmarking and make it difficult to compare rates of retention and achievement across the different delivery routes.

2.10 These arrangements do not help deliver the consistent and co-ordinated approaches or the proper evidence base necessary to drive forward our agenda for raising standards. Nor do they establish the clear accountability necessary for ensuring quality. The case for integration and harmonisation is compelling.

Why structural change is necessary

2.11 This is the case for change. There is too much duplication, confusion and bureaucracy in the current system. Too little money actually reaches learners and employers, too much is tied up in bureaucracy. There is an absence of effective co-ordination or strategic planning. The system has insufficient focus on skill and employer needs at national, regional and local levels. The system lacks innovation and flexibility, and there needs to be more collaboration and co-operation to ensure higher standards and the right range of choices. We need to exploit the potential of information and communication technology both in the way provision is planned and in the way it is delivered and we need to make it readily and easily available to those who want to learn. Measured against the principles set out in *The Learning Age*, the current system falls short. It is incapable of delivering the improvements needed to achieve our goals.

The objectives of change

2.12 The Government's aim is to create in partnership a framework of opportunities for learning; to remove the barriers which prevent people from taking advantage of these opportunities; and to maximise the benefit from the significant amount of public investment we put into post-16 education and training. Improvements in attainment and enhanced employability will result. Our objectives are to:

- **promote excellence**. People have a right to expect that the provision they receive is of the highest quality, as do employers investing in the skills of their workforce. Much current post-16 education and training is of good quality, but all provision must meet these standards;

- **give employers a substantial stake in shaping what is provided in post-16 education and training**. The new arrangements must respond flexibly and rapidly to the changing needs of the labour market, supplying that mix of qualifications which best meets the skills needed by employers in the workplace;

- **create systems which are driven by and responsive to the needs of individuals, businesses and their communities**. Funding should follow individuals and employers and the wider community should decide the mix of opportunities which are made available, so as to meet the needs of local, regional and national labour markets and reflect the wishes of local communities. Improved employability will be the result;

- **give everyone access to education, training and skills opportunities**. Systems should be equitable and inclusive. Funding arrangements should take account of the extra cost of meeting the needs of the most vulnerable groups. Those who lack basic skills, or who require particular help in other areas, may require flexible and innovative approaches. There should be a commitment to mainstreaming equal opportunities throughout policy making, implementation and service delivery;

- **ensure people have access to support**. Good quality information and advice should be available to everyone. We must improve access to education and training and make it easier to find out about the range of opportunities available;

- **design systems which deliver efficiency**. We must cut out fragmentation, bureaucracy and duplication. By reducing waste and increasing value for money we will release resources and deliver improvements that benefit the learner;

- **improve accountability and probity**. This should be delivered at all levels through the system; providers should be looking to set new standards which are a model for other sectors; and

- **change in a evolutionary way**. We should build on what works well now and ensure continuity and progression towards achieving targets.

2.13 The proposals that follow in this White Paper are rooted in this analysis of the need for change and designed to acheive the objectives set out above.

CHAPTER 3

The Learning and Skills Council

3.1 Our vision for a learning society requires radical reform and modernisation of the current delivery arrangements for post-16 learning. We propose to establish a new framework, capable of tackling the serious weaknesses of the existing systems and building on the successes of the present arrangements, including the significant involvement of business in the shaping of provision.

3.2 We propose to create a new Learning and Skills Council for England. It will be responsible for strategic development, planning, funding, management and quality assurance of post-16 education and training (excluding higher education). The new Council's remit will include further education, community and adult learning, work-based training for young people, workforce development, and information, advice, guidance and support for adults. The Council's role in relation to school sixth forms is discussed in Chapter 6.

3.3 The Council will assume responsibility for funding for: FE sector colleges from the FEFC; Government funded training and workforce development from TECs; and adult and community learning from local authorities. It will also assume responsibility for advising the Government on the National Learning Targets from the National Advisory Council for Education and Training Targets (NACETT). Its primary function will be to meet the learning needs of businesses, individuals and communities by putting in place a consistent and coherent system of funding.

3.4 The new body, once established, is expected to have responsibility for a budget of around £5 billion and the education and training opportunities of over five million adults and young people.

3.5 Subject to the passage of legislation, the Council will be established in April 2001. It will be set up as an executive Non-Departmental Public Body (NDPB).

Functions of the new Learning and Skills Council

3.6 The Council will advise the Government on future National Learning Targets. It will also be responsible for setting a learning and skills strategy for achieving all post-16 Learning Targets, working with the Higher Education Funding Council for England in respect of the targets at degree level. It will work closely with the Ufl at a local and national level, in carrying out its functions.

3.7 The Council's functions will include:

- ensuring that high quality post-16 provision is available to meet the needs of employers, individuals and communities;

- planning the coherent provision and funding of institutions, private and voluntary sector providers, and planning for mergers where appropriate;

- developing of national funding tariffs and systems, for the great majority of its expenditure;

- direct responsibility for the achievement of targets for: young people; for adults (excluding level 4 for which prime responsibility will continue to rest with the HE sector); and for Investors in People;

- promoting and supporting social partnership strategies, working with others to raise the aspirations and achievements of young people and adults for learning;

- promoting equality of opportunity and ensuring that the needs of the most disadvantaged in the labour market are best met;

- promoting programmes and policies such as Modern Apprenticeships, National Traineeships and Investors in People;

- ensuring an effective Education Business Partnership network exists to support the delivery of work-related learning (including providing experience of work) for those aged under 16, and so complement post-16 provision;

- funding information, advice and guidance for adults;

- establishing systems for the collection and dissemination of information on labour market and skill trends to improve the basis on which markets work and decisions are taken; and

- ensuring value for money and financial propriety, regularity and control, intervening early and effectively where necessary and ensuring that there are sound arrangements for governance, financial management and audit throughout the post-16 sector.

3.8   In delivering its functions, the Learning and Skills Council will need to work with a wide range of partners. The Council will also need to build into its work the recommendations of the national Skills Task Force. This was set up in February 1998 to assist the Government in developing a National Skills Agenda. The Skills Task Force has produced two reports and is due to conclude its work in March 2000. The Government will consider at that point how best to take forward its work with the aim of ensuring that the Learning and Skills Council will continue to have access to the authoritative and innovative thinking on skills issues that the Task Force has provided.

Membership of the new Council

3.9   The Council's members will be drawn from people with relevant experience. The vast majority will be drawn from those representing the consumers of education and skills - from employers (large and small), people involved in lifelong learning, and from other community and individual interests, such as local government, the voluntary sector, trade unions and providers of information, advice and guidance. Employers will form the largest single group and will, directly influence a far wider range of post-16 provision, than they do now, covering academic as well as vocational education. This will deliver a strong customer influence in the new arrangements and ensure that the business sector continues to have a significant say in decisions about provision. There will also be members - representing the 'supply' side - with an education or training background. We propose a Council consisting of a Chair and around 15 members who will be appointed, using national advertisements, by the Secretary of State for Education and Employment.

The Committees of the Council

3.10 In order to raise participation and attainment among young people and adults, provision must be relevant to and support their learning needs and priorities. We propose that the Council is supported and advised by two Committees with direct responsibility respectively for young people (generally pre-19) and adult learners. The Committees will consist of members who have a real understanding of the needs of each group. They will be responsible for using information in a consistent, focused and forward looking way to identify and assess the needs of their group and current and future labour market skills. The Committees will advise the Learning and Skills Council who will use it to form the basis for the strategies, plans and funding decisions, including the allocation of funds and the development and implementation of funding systems.

3.11 The Secretary of State's annual remit letter to the Council will set indicative budgets for the client groups of the two Committees. Within these budgets, each Committee will be responsible for advising the Learning and Skills Council, in relation to its relevant groups, on:

- the range and level of provision necessary to meet their needs;

- measures to improve the standards and quality of provision;

- measures to promote excellence, social inclusion and equality of opportunity;

- measures to increase participation and retention; and

- the funding tariffs and systems required to give effect to their advice and encourage responsiveness to learning and skill needs.

Young People's Learning Committee

3.12 The Young People's Learning Committee will be responsible for advising the national Council on the best means of achieving of the National Learning Targets for young people including strategies for increasing participation and attainment so that as many young people as possible continue in learning until the age of 19. The Committees will also be expected to ensure that young people learn in ways which improve their employability and contribute to their personal development. The specific responsibilities of the Young People's Learning Committee will include advising the Learning and Skills Council on the effective funding and delivery of:

- GCE A and AS Levels, GNVQs, NVQs and other education and work based training provision targeted specifically at pre-19 year olds;

- Modern Apprenticeships and National Traineeships. Although these go beyond age 19, they would more appropriately be placed within the responsibility of this Committee;

- the promotion and support of work-related learning, including activities providing experience of work, for those aged under 16; and

- the successful transition of young people into the next stage of education, training or work, including any measures to engage all young people in learning and to promote progression into higher education where this is appropriate.

3.13 The Young People's Learning Committee will work alongside a new support service for young people which we propose to establish; our proposals are set out in Chapter 6. The Committee will also need to work closely with representatives of young people, their parents, schools, colleges and other providers to ensure that provision best meets the needs of students. And it will be important to ensure that its decisions are informed by an understanding of the present and future needs of employers and business. This will include working closely with employers including National Training Organisations to ensure effective delivery of skill needs. Close links with the Employment Service will also help integrate learning up to the age of 19 with the skill elements of New Deal for Young People.

The Adult Learning Committee

3.14 The Adult Learning Committee will have direct responsibility for advising the Learning and Skills Council on achieving the National Learning Targets for adults and for organisations (specifically the Targets for Investors in People). This will include advising on raising and widening participation and attainment of adults. The Committee will look at issues of accessibility, working closely with the Small Business Service to encourage businesses to invest in their workforce through learning and development. It will advise on ways in which the transition for those who return to learning can be made less traumatic in order to reduce drop-out rates for returners. The Committee will be expected to focus on addressing basic skills issues (which the UfI will also treat as an initial priority in the development of materials and support).

3.15 The primary function of the Adult Learning Committee will be to meet and match the learning needs of individuals, businesses and communities. Its specific responsibilities will include advising the Learning and Skills Council on the effective funding and delivery of:

- adult education and training in further education colleges;

- adult learning at home and in the community;

- workforce development including the promotion of NVQs, and Investors in People - the Committee will also need to work closely with the Young People's Learning Committee on Modern Apprenticeships and National Apprenticeships as these form an important element of policies for workforce development;

- more flexible access to learning e.g. to encourage participation amongst people with family responsibilities; and

- information, advice and guidance for adults.

3.16 The Adult Learning Committee will also need to work closely with the Employment Service over the provision of work based learning for adults, and in particular New Deal for the over 25s; with National Training Organisations in meeting sectoral needs; with the UfI over the development and delivery of work based learning, with Chambers of Commerce, with the higher education sector and with the voluntary sector.

Employers and the Learning and Skills Council

3.17 Employers have a major contribution to make to the success of the Learning and Skills Council at national and local level. Their role will include:

- ensuring that national strategies and plans are realistic, reflect trends in the labour market and deliver the skills that employers' need;

- at local level, identifying skill shortages and gaps in provision and adjusting the national tarriff price accordingly so that supply meets demand;

- at local level, making good links between providers and employers to facilitate sectoral initiatives. An example is in Birmingham where the TEC has developed a manufacturing skills initiative in the vehicles sector. This involves all the major motor vehicle manufacturers in the Birmingham and Coventry area who have come together to identify skill needs and establish a preferred supplier scheme among local colleges to develop an effective supply side response; and

- providing places for Modern Apprenticeships and National Traineeships and promoting Investors in People recognitions. Successful TECs have developed these national initiatives as part of a wider focus on business development. Close links will be necessary to the new Small Business Service.

Coherence with pre-16 learning

3.18 Ensuring the successful transition of young people from pre to post-16 learning and onto the next stage of education, training or work will be critical if the new arrangements are to succeed. The Learning and Skills Council must build on the work already done to promote progression for all 14-19 year olds, particularly those who have previously been turned off by learning. Currently, schools have flexibility at Key Stage 4 to enhance opportunities for work related learning. Our proposals for a revised national curriculum from 2000 extend this approach and will provide wider opportunities, as will the *Qualifying for Success* reforms announced earlier this year which will increase the opportunities for young people to pursue a broader post-16 curriculum. We want to build on the best practice in schools, further and higher education and work based provision. There should be enough flexibility in the curriculum to allow options for those who are not motivated by a traditional curriculum offering and would find other options, such as the more vocational route, attractive. This will include schemes whereby disaffected and excluded 14-16 year old pupils are able to study in colleges and with voluntary sector providers in conjunction with employers.

3.19 We would expect the Learning and Skills Council to seek further ways of enhancing opportunities for young people to be able to study in flexible ways that suit their needs. The Council will do this in part through the promotion and support of work experience programmes for those aged under 16. It will work to build on the contribution of all those involved in Education Business Partnerships, including local education authorities, to ensure coherence between school business links for pre-16 education and the post-16 agenda.

Question: *What more might we do to ensure coherence between the work of the Learning and Skills Council and pre-16 learning?*

Local Learning and Skills Councils

3.20 Planning and funding decisions taken by the Learning and Skills Council must respond to the skills and learning needs of local labour markets and communities. Without a strong understanding of these needs, we will not achieve the responsiveness or sensitivity needed. Effective linkage of local labour market needs to local provision will also help to drive forward improvements in quality. We propose that the Learning and Skills Council operates through a network of 40-50 local Learning and Skills Councils. These would be arms of the national Council, to ensure that we achieve the right blend of provision needed for local areas.

Role of local Learning and Skills Councils

3.21 The local Councils will take responsibility for raising standards and for securing provision to match local learning and skills needs. It will be important that they have sufficient flexibility and discretion, and our proposals for securing this are described in Chapter 4.

3.22 Local Councils will be responsible - with the support of local Learning Partnerships - for:

- assembling comprehensive data for their areas on the characteristics of client groups, in particular, rates of participation in learning and the relative performance of providers in terms of value added, value for money and success in achieving skills and qualifications;

- drawing up an assessment of local skill needs for their area in consultation with key local and regional partners (including the local Learning Partnerships, Ufl and the Regional Development Agencies). These assessments will need to draw on and in turn support the regional economic strategies developed by RDAs in close consultation with regional and economic partners. The assessments will require on-going dialogue with employers as well as individual and community interests;

- on the basis of this data and assessment, as well as inspection and audit reports, publishing an 'annual statement of priorities' for their areas i.e. a targeted action plan to set out the key challenges and objectives covering post-16 education and training in their area. This plan would be set within the national framework, priorities and guidance provided by the national Learning and Skills Council and the Government. It would set out the local Council's proposals for meeting local and regional needs, for improving the quality and cost-effectiveness of provision, for promoting excellence and equality of opportunity in education and training locally, and for widening access particularly for those people who face disadvantage in the labour market because of their race, disability, gender or age. The plan would also set out how the local Council would foster effective links between schools and businesses. Each plan will be approved by the national Council, having consulted the relevant RDA;

- managing a discretionary budget which will be used to address local learning and skills issues by encouraging and supporting, for example new approaches, to workforce development, particularly in SMEs, or to promote improved delivery arrangements where appropriate; and

- working with business to expand the availability and take up of Modern Apprenticeships, National Traineeships and other Government supported training from local employers and for promoting and marketing Investors in People and workforce development programmes to employers.

3.23 The local Councils will also be responsible for:

- ensuring a fair and competitive market which new providers are encouraged to enter, provided they meet agreed quality standards;

- developing local delivery plans in conjunction with the local Learning Partnerships, Education Business Partnerships, local education authorities, and others responsible for providing education and training. These plans would set out priorities for improving the quality, value for money and effectiveness of local provision;

- developing an overall quality improvement strategy. This is described in more detail in Chapter 5. Within this framework, the local Learning and Skills Council will be responsible for assuring itself of the quality, standards and probity of bodies it funds. The local council will also ensure concerns about the quality of provision are investigated promptly and thoroughly. Where area wide provision is found to be weak or failing by the area-wide inspection proposed in Chapter 5, the local Council will respond with appropriate proposals for reform and improvement;

- proposing college and other provider mergers and helping broker them at a local level - within a national policy framework set by the national Council;

- focusing local provision more closely on customer needs, for example, through opening up colleges or training centres in the evenings and all year round for the benefit of individuals and employers; and

- providing fair and accurate information on the range of opportunities in their area, together with objective assessments of the quality of provision. This might form the basis of an annual 'prospectus' of post-16 opportunities, to be given to all young people as they approach 16 by the independent service which will advise and support them in the choices they make (see chapter 6).

Question: Are the proposed responsibilities of the local Learning and Skills Council the right ones to ensure responsiveness at local level to the needs of local labour markets and communities?

Membership

3.24 The local Councils' membership will be broadly along the lines of the national Council but will reflect the diversity of local business and the wider community interest. This will be essential to ensure that the local Council can be influenced by, and respond to, the needs of the local labour market. They will have significant business involvement and, as in the National Council, employers will form the largest single group. Membership will also reflect the trade unions and the social economy, being able to represent the needs of the local employment interests both employers and trades unions, as well as local Learning Partnerships. The Chairs will be influential people in their local area, appointed by the Secretary of State after seeking advice from the national Learning and Skills Council. The members will be appointed by the national Council following open advertisements. Each local Council will have an Executive Director responsible to the local Board.

Establishing the boundaries and coverage

3.25 The Government does not intend to impose rigid conformity on the size and number of these local Learning and Skills Councils. However, it proposes a set of principles which should underpin decisions about their structure. Boundaries should so far as possible reflect or be consistent with those of other key organisations. This will facilitate planning, co-ordination, and joined up working. It will also be essential that the planning and purchasing role is carried out close enough to local markets to be sensitive to local needs. It is this balance that has led us to believe that we would expect no more than 50 local Councils. We will ask Regional Development Agencies and the London Development Partnership to make proposals by the end of September 1999 for the boundaries of the local Learning and Skills Councils - in consultation with key local and regional partners - taking account of the following key considerations.

3.26 Boundaries should:

- fit with local travel-to-work and travel-to-study patterns and with the pattern of business and commercial activities;

- be co-terminous with other key local economic or social units and partnerships - especially with local authorities, the local outlets of the Small Business Service, the sub-regional partnerships set up locally to tackle economic and social issues, and be within Regional Development Agencies/Government Offices boundaries; and

- be large enough to assure economies of scale and cost effectiveness - we consider a resident population of 0.5 million to be the minimum - although we expect this to be much greater in conurbations.

Chart showing organisation of Learning and Skills Council

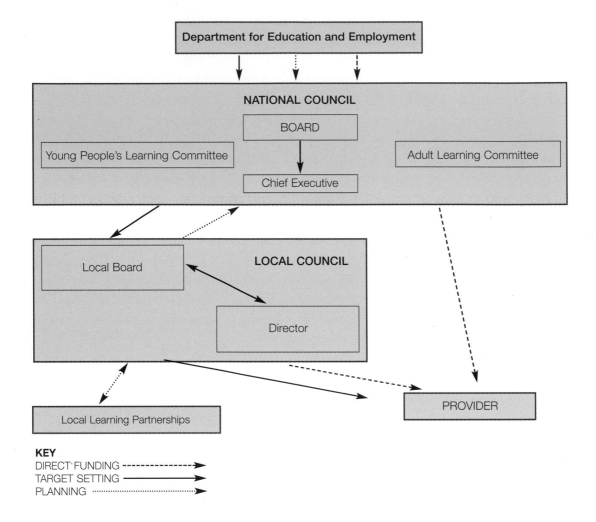

Local Learning Partnerships

3.27 We have been impressed by the enthusiasm of a wide range of organisations to work together within the local Learning Partnerships. We want to build on their efforts. Local Learning Partnerships have a key role in driving forward improvements in the quality of provision and bringing greater coherence at the local level. Working together, partners can identify and address gaps in provision, eliminate duplication and co-ordinate local action to raise achievement - making sure that it meets local needs. It will therefore be essential that local Learning Partnerships are placed at the heart of the new arrangements and that we build on the momentum we have already achieved in setting up a national Learning Partnership network. The whole system must be driven from the bottom up - and the local Learning Partnerships will have the key responsibility for delivering this.

3.28 It will be critical that the local Learning and Skills Councils work with the local Learning Partnerships. We envisage a strong and important role for the Learning Partnerships within a 'family' of organisations - not a 'hierachy' - working together to meet the learning and skills needs of their local community. However, it will be important that each organisation has a specific role and focus, to avoid duplication of effort and to ensure that they add value. We see the Learning Partnerships acting as a catalyst for collaborative action at the local level and ensuring co-ordination of efforts.

3.29 Currently local Learning Partnerships have responsibility for driving forward action on the post-16 National Learning Targets for 2002. They will continue with this vital task. When the Learning and Skills Council comes into operation, in 2001, it will be directly responsible to the Government for the achievement of all relevant targets. An early task will therefore be to take stock with local Learning Partnerships of progress made in their area and any further steps necessary to reach the targets. In due course, as the National Learning Targets are set for the years after 2002, the Learning and Skills Council will advise the Government on what these targets should be and will then work with local Learning Partnerships to translate them into what makes sense locally, and to develop delivery plans to achieve them.

3.30 Local Learning Partnerships include - as a core - colleges, TECs, local authorities and careers service. But many also include employers, the voluntary and community sector, schools, higher education institutions and the Employment Service. Their strength is their detailed knowledge of their area, of the local labour market and of the causes and social conditions which underlie the extent of participation in education and training. We want the Partnerships to develop this role further so that they draw in a wide range of representatives of the local learning market - including learners themselves. In developing and broadening their membership in this way, the local Learning Partnerships will be able to help ensure that the local Learning and Skills Council accounts effectively to its local communities. For example, the local Learning and Skills Council might regularly present its plans and performance reports to the local Learning Partnership as part of its arrangements to account for its performance. Our proposals on accountability are discussed further in para 3.34.

3.31 The local Council will look to the Learning Partnership for advice on a range of issues. These will include:

- planning and delivering strategies to maximise the participation of young people in learning, in particular through the new Learning Gateway;

- providing a voice for local businesses creating opportunities for local business people to influence provision in their area;

- strengthening the work of Education Business Partnerships;

- drawing upon detailed local knowledge to advise on economic development issues; and

- building local flexibility into the overall planning and funding arrangements, so as to meet best the needs of the local area.

3.32 We see an important new role for the local Learning Partnerships in establishing a forum for learners in which their feedback can help improve the quality of provision. Experience from New Start which has shown that setting up a Youth Forum enables young people to advise constructively on local arrangements. We propose that local Learning Partnerships support such Forums to help advise the Council on the above issues.

3.33 The local Learning and Skills Councils will also want to build on the work that Partnerships have already started to play in local provision for adult and community learning. Here too, the knowledge and experience of the Partnerships will be crucial. It includes the vital role of Partnerships in developing and improving arrangements for adult basic skills provision and for putting in place coherent arrangements for local information, advice and guidance for adults.

Questions: *Are the functions described for the local Learning Partnerships the right ones to build on the momentum already generated? How can the local Learning Partnerships best work with and support the local Learning and Skills Councils?*

Ensuring accountability

3.34 We are committed to making public services more effective and accountable. In introducing the new arrangements set out in this White Paper, it will be essential that those responsible for delivering them account effectively and in an open and transparent way for their performance. It is a key aim of the new arrangements that we will achieve improved accountability and openness at both the national and the local level. We want to build on the good practice which exists within the current system, of which there are many examples. This includes the TEC National Council's framework for local accountability which was approved by the Nolan Committee as a model of good practice. The FEFC has also adopted codes of conduct for its members and staff, and holds an annual open meeting which the public may attend. Many further education colleges have implemented similar arrangements, and from this autumn the Government's new measures designed to increase accountability to stakeholders will apply.

Accountability to Parliament

3.35 The Learning and Skills Council will be fully accountable to Ministers and Parliament. The Chief Executive of the Learning and Skills Council will be the Accounting Officer. The National Audit Office will be the auditor and will have inspection rights to the Council. Additionally, Parliamentary Select Committees will have the right to scrutinise any aspect of the Learning and Skills Council's performance.

Accountability to its customers

3.36 The Learning and Skills Council must be fully accountable to its customers and stakeholders, at national and local level. It will adopt the seven principles of public life - established by the Nolan Committee - selflessness; integrity; objectivity; accountability; openness; honesty; and leadership. It will also be responsible for ensuring that there is a sound framework for evaluating the systems of financial management, control, governance and value for money in the bodies which it funds.

3.37 Key features of the accountability framework which we will develop will include:

- the publication of business and corporate plans (for both the national Council and for the local Learning and Skills Councils), which will include strategic objectives, performance indicators, and how these will be evaluated - and the publication of an annual report and annual accounts;

- arrangements for publishing regular performance information as well as an annual report and accounts;

- arrangements for consulting customers and for receiving and responding to concerns raised. The Council will be expected to meet the Citizen's Charter Standards;

- holding periodic open meetings at national and local level wherever appropriate involving the wider community in its activities;

- the use of a website at national and local level, and other media where appropriate to provide information on its services and performance;

- making the Council subject to the Government's proposed Freedom of Information Act;

- the Learning and Skills Council will adopt a Board Members code, which will be based on the Code of Best Practice for Board Members of Public Bodies and will include a register of members interests; and

- the publication of a 'management statement' which will set out the role and organisation of the Council; its aim and objectives; arrangements for managing health and safety; the respective roles and the accountability of the Chairman, Board Members, and Chief Executive; and its relationship with DfEE.

Openness at local level

3.38 The local Learning and Skills Councils will also be expected to involve their area community when drawing up their plans and in monitoring progress. They will, in their day to day business, demonstrate that they are developing ways of improving accountability to their local communities. In particular, they must publicise what they are doing and invite comment.

Handling complaints

3.39 We would expect the Learning and Skills Council to establish and publish an effective complaints procedure at national and local level covering both the operation of the Council itself and the learning it secures. Care will be taken to ensure that this process has sufficient independence to provide reassurance to students and others. This process will provide early warning of emerging issues and ensure people receive the high quality service they have the right to expect. We would also expect the Learning and Skills Council to publish an analysis of complaints received and action taken.

Question: What more can we do to ensure accountability at local and national level?

CHAPTER 4

A framework for success beyond 16

4.1 Current arrangements - as described in Chapter 2 - are incoherent in planning post-16 education and training, and inconsistent and over-complex in its funding. We have an opportunity in building a new system to simplify arrangements and make it easier for providers and employers to engage with the system and for learners to benefit from it.

4.2 The new arrangements that we are setting in place will not only increase the transparency and simplicity of the systems but will cut out many of the layers which have developed in the existing systems. We will reduce bureaucracy and improve efficiency by greater standardisation, with common IT, finance and administration systems. The effect of these changes will be to reduce financial overheads, releasing those resources for the provision of front line services. In 1997-98, TEC accounts showed an average of 13% of total income was spent on administrative costs, varying between TECs from 6% to 35%. For comparison, under 1% of the FEFC's budgets went on administration and inspection.

4.3 This chapter sets out the goals of a new planning and funding system, how it will work in practice and how we will measure success. It then explains the way in which the Learning and Skills Council will work with its partners - in particular the UfI, the Regional Development Agencies, the Local Education Authorities, the local Learning Partnerships, and National Training Organisations to plan more effective provision which will better support higher participation and improved attainment and skills.

Goals for a new planning and funding system

4.4 The new planning and funding system will:

- promote excellence and high quality delivery of service;

- maximise participation, retention and achievement towards the National Learning Targets for 2002 and beyond;

- be responsive to the needs of individuals and employers;

- promote employability for individuals by equipping them with skills in demand in the labour market;

- ensure targetted support for the socially disadvantaged;

- ensure equality of opportunity;

- secure the entitlement for all 16-19 year olds to stay in learning;

- remove unnecessary bureaucracy; and

- secure maximum effectiveness and value for money.

4.5   To achieve these goals, the Learning and Skills Council will need comprehensive data to track individual students and learners so as to draw out patterns of retention, attainment, efficiency and effectiveness by different sectors. The Council will also need soundly based systems of customer feedback and plans for national and local evaluation.

4.6   A key function of the Learning and Skills Council will be to develop and apply a new funding system. This will be demand-focused, reflecting the needs of individuals, employers and communities and will be based on a tariff system - providing a clear national basis for the funding of different qualifications - which will cover the vast majority of funding for further education and training. The funding system will build on the strengths of the current FEFC tariff system, which has promoted considerable growth in further education at relatively modest bureaucratic cost. But the Council will need to take a first principles approach to ensure that the system it devises adequately caters for future requirements of post-16 learners, however and wherever they study: whether on courses leading to formal qualifications or in more informal adult and community education; and whether registered at a college or studying independently, e.g. like some Ufl learners, in the home or in the workplace.

4.7   The new funding system should also be designed to meet skill needs in the economy at local, regional and national levels. Developing the right funding regime will be an early priority for the new Council. To provide a base for that, we want to learn from the experience of those who have worked within the current systems, with all their strengths and weaknesses. We therefore propose to consult on the key elements of a new funding system with partners later in the year. This system will need to include consideration of ways in which we can build in local flexibility where appropriate. It will also need to promote equality of opportunity and meet the needs of people who face particular disadvantages in the labour market.

Ensuring local flexibility and autonomy

4.8   The local Learning and Skills Councils will need sufficient discretion to secure the right balance and mix of post-16 provision within their area. This is critical if we are to deliver a system which better matches skills to the evolving occupational requirements of employers and reduce the damaging impact of skill shortages. Giving the local Councils an element of discretion will also be central to attracting high quality candidates to serve on their Boards, particularly from the business community. It will therefore be important to get the balance right between local flexibility and discretion and securing the benefits of greater consistency and standardisation through a national framework. One way of doing so would be to allow local Councils some flexibility within the national funding tariffs, subject to clear limits set by the national Council. That could help meet local needs for occupations where particular skill shortages had been identified or where there were gaps in provision for the socially excluded. Local Councils would need to justify the use of any flexibility by demonstrating its effectiveness in meeting skill needs and filling gaps in the provision of learning opportunities, working with local Learning Partnerships.

4.9   Other examples of areas where there will be local flexibility and discretion will be:

- **quality improvement:** local Learning and Skills Councils will monitor the quality of provision in their area; and where the inspection process reveals weaknesses or failure, they will use funds to help drive improvements. They will also encourage networks of providers to share good practice and collaborate on quality improvement initiatives;

- **building capacity within the market:** the funding system needs to be flexible enough to enable a greater variety of provision and providers to be funded - for example to encourage 'first rung' or 'taster' provision which gets people back into the learning habit; or the development of learning centres and learning hubs, for example, through the UfI;

- **adult and community learning:** we will establish a planning system that involves the local Learning Partnerships and which will ensure that funding is targeted on identified community needs (see Chapter 7 for further details);

- **Education Business Partnerships:** the local Learning and Skills Councils will take over responsibility from TECs for budgets to support work experience and teacher placements' and to promote effective local involvement of business in education;

- **Investors in People:** working closely with the Small Business Service in respect of small and medium sized employers and with Investors in People (UK), the local Learning and Skills Councils will have responsibility for funds to support employers to become recognised as Investors in People;

- **discretionary funding:** to enable the local Learning and Skills Councils to identify and meet local needs and to fund innovative projects, possibly in partnership with other bodies such as the Small Business Service.

Question: Is there more we should do to ensure we strike the right balance between national arrangements and local flexibility and discretion?

Ensuring integration with other funds

4.10 The local Learning and Skills Councils' annual plans will take account of all the public funding available for post-16 education and training within their area. Employers themselves carry the main responsibility for investing in the training of their people and local Learning and Skills Councils will seek to create the maximum synergy between this investment and the public funds at their disposal. It will also be important that they build on the significant progress made by TECs to secure and maximise employer contributions to Government funded training.

4.11 There are also sources of public funding apart from its own funds which the local Learning and Skills Council will need to build into its plans in a coherent and co-ordinated way so as to maximise the local impact. These include the Single Regeneration Budget (SRB) and the European Social and Regional Development Funds. The European Social Fund (ESF) in particular makes a significant contribution to the achievement of the Government's education and training priorities, improving the employment prospects of those who are most disadvantaged in the labour market. In 1999 approximately £1 billion is available to the UK through the European Social Fund.

4.12 The new ESF Regulation for the period 2000 to 2006 requires a link to be made between the ESF and the priorities set out in the UK Employment Action Plan. Preparation for the new programme also provides the opportunity to examine and improve the interface between domestic and European funding regimes. It will be essential to ensure that in developing a new funding and planning system the effectiveness of ESF support is maximised. In particular:

- ESF funds must be planned and targeted in a way which adds value to and complements post-16 education and training provision funded through the Learning and Skills Council. The effective use of ESF funding will be a central part of the plans drawn up by the local Learning and Skills Councils. We will also expect ESF bids which cover proposals involving post-16 education and training to demonstrate how they fit within the Learning and Skills Council local plans and priorities;

- funding arrangements must support access to ESF. Bringing greater integration of public funding for post-16 provision under the Learning and Skills Council will make it easier for applicants to gain access to suitable match-funding and minimise scope for double funding.

Question: How can we ensure that the arrangements ensure integration of all the public funding available within the area?

Funding and planning provision for people with special needs

4.13 Part of the Government's commitment to equality of opportunity is to ensure that planning and funding arrangements result in adequate support so that students with disabilities and special needs, from specific learning difficulties to severe and profound challenges, can achieve their full potential. The bringing together of post-16 education and training provides a unique opportunity to integrate different approaches and improve arrangements for the benefit of learners. This will build on and extend the progress made by further education colleges in recent years in provision for such students.

4.14 The Government will ensure that the new arrangements are based on the principles of the Tomlinson Committee's report to the FEFC, "Inclusive Learning", and the examples of good practice in TEC-funded provision, particularly by a number of voluntary organisations.

4.15 The Learning and Skills Council will have a particular duty to address the needs of learners with disabilities or learning difficulties, including consulting with voluntary and specialist organisations and representative and user groups on how best to make suitable provision available and then drawing up appropriate funding and planning arrangements. It will have the power to fund specialist provision, including residential provision, outside the adult and further education sectors for students over compulsory school age with learning difficulties or disabilities. This may be appropriate where the Council is satisfied that facilities available in institutions within the further and adult education sector are not adequate to meet the needs of a particular individual or where it is in the best interests of an individual student to do so. In deciding whether external specialist provision is appropriate, the Council will also be mindful of the quality and suitability of provision offered by alternative institutions. The Council will have the power to agree joint funding for a student, for example with a social services department, health authority, local education authority or other body where appropriate. The current legal duties on local authorities to fund the care of those with profound learning difficulties or disabilities will remain unchanged.

4.16 In addition, it will be important to ensure that there are effective arrangements in place for the transition of young people with special educational needs from school into further education or employment. This transition is a challenge for all young people, but those with special needs face additional difficulties. Current arrangements, which involve the development of a transition plan at age 14 for children with a statement and which allocate clear responsibility for the different aspects of the young person's development, will continue to underpin provision for such students in the new arrangements. It will also be important to ensure effective arrangements for the transition of other young people who are vulnerable, for example young people in the care of the local authority, but who may not be the subject of a statement.

Question: How can we ensure that the planning and funding arrangements support people with special needs?

Measuring success

4.17 Improving standards and effectiveness requires that regular information is available and applied in reviewing and evaluating performance against objectives. Setting clear targets and performance indicators which measure outputs, outcomes and impact will be critical to this. The Learning and Skills Council will therefore set up systems that evaluate how well they:

- **meet the needs of individuals and employers and thereby encourage investment in training.** The new arrangements must address skills needs at national and local level; be responsive to the changing needs of employers; support and encourage employer participation and contribution to the cost of learning; and meet the aspirations of individuals;

- **promote lifelong learning**. Increasing and widening levels of participation in education and training for people of all ages;

- **drive up standards of provision**;

- are **adaptable and responsive to local and community needs.** The new arrangements must keep at their heart the needs of the communities they serve;

- provide clear **accountability for the achievement of the National Learning Targets**. the Learning and Skills Council will be accountable for the achievement of all post-16 National Learning Targets;

- **help tackle social exclusion and promote equal opportunity**. This will include helping unemployed people to improve their employability, ensuring equality of opportunity for all, through education and training and enabling students with disabilities and special needs to achieve their full potential; and

- **improve efficiency and effectiveness**. By cutting out fragmentation, bureaucracy and duplication within the existing system the new arrangements will reduce waste, increase value for money and deliver improved effectiveness.

Question: Are these the right set of critical success factors against which to evaluate the new arrangements?

Working in partnership

4.18 To achieve its objectives, the Learning and Skills Council - and its local arms - will need to develop close and effective links with a range of organisations at national, regional and local levels.

The Regional Development Agencies (RDAs)

4.19 RDAs are responsible for developing and overseeing the implementation of the Regional Economic Strategy, within which their skills strategy will form an important and integral element. In addition, each RDA has a statutory duty "to enhance the development and application of skills relevant to employment in its area" and each has its own Skills Development Fund to help meet priority skills needs. The Government wants to ensure that there is a strong link between the RDAs and the Learning and Skills Council both at national and local level. Learning and skills training should be planned to reflect the needs and priorities of the region set out in the RDA's regional strategy, and performance against the regional plan should be monitored. This should be a two-way process - the RDA equally will be influenced by the Learning and Skills Council in preparing and updating its strategy.

4.20 It will be important that the Learning and Skills Council and RDAs work together to:

- share labour market information and economic assessments to ensure plans are developed on a consistent basis;

- ensure that the plans of the local Learning and Skills Councils are drawn up with reference to the regional strategy; and

- ensure that the National Skills Agenda is informed by regional priorities.

4.21 To achieve this RDAs will:

- identify sectors of key importance to the region and give guidance accordingly, drawing on NTOs' knowledge of sectoral skills needs, to enable the Learning and Skills Council to respond to such demand;

- assess local plans and advise the national Council to ensure that they are consistent with overall plans for regional strategies and to raise any issues or concerns;

- work with the local Learning and Skills Councils to assess the achievement of their regional skills strategies and priorities locally;

- be represented on the local Learning and Skills Councils and on the national Council; and

- work closely with the Learning and Skills Council, relevant NTOs and local partners on developing skills packages for regional inward investment programmes.

4.22 The relationship between the Learning and Skills Council and the London Development Partnership and, following its launch on 3rd July 2000, the London Development Agency (LDA) will reflect that outlined above.

Local authorities

4.23 Local authorities plan and fund much post-16 provision, particularly in school sixth forms and this role will broadly continue under the new arrangements. Local authorities also have a comprehensive view of their local communities and a strategic and key role to play in tackling issues of social exclusion. Some already play a lead part in bringing together local service providers through the New Commitment to Regeneration pathfinders to develop area wide strategies for regeneration. They are also involved in other regeneration partnerships, such as New Deal for Communities and SRB.

4.24 Through representation on the local Learning and Skills Councils and as key partners in the local Learning Partnerships, the new arrangements for post-16 learning will give them greater influence over a broad range of education and training opportunities than they have at present through their limited role on TEC Boards. Learning and Skills Councils will be able to support the regeneration role of local authorities through tailored local education, training and business-focused initiatives.

Ufl

4.25 The objectives of the Ufl are to stimulate demand for lifelong learning among businesses and individuals and to improve access to relevant, high quality learning opportunities. Its approach is founded on a learner-centred set of principles which seek to maximise individual choice and flexibility by providing clear information and advice (through the Learning Direct service, for which Ufl is responsible), innovative and relevant learning materials, and specialist support. The Ufl will enable people to learn at home, in the workplace and in learning centres. A network of Ufl-endorsed learning centres, based in a wide range of locations, including colleges, libraries, community centres, employers' premises, and shopping malls, will provide public access to Ufl learning materials, learning services and ICT facilities. The Ufl will build on and extend the use of interactive learning, terrestrial, satellite and digital television and the broader opportunities of technology to widen access to learning. The Ufl has been established as an independent company limited by guarantee in order to give it the commercial freedom and operational flexibility it needs.

4.26 The objectives and approach of the Ufl - which is working towards a full national launch in autumn 2000 - are complementary to the new Learning and Skills Council. In particular the Learning and Skills Council will be able to benefit from the Ufl approach to flexible and distributed learning and from its plans to engage more learners at home and in learning centres in the workplace. It will be important to build in from the start effective joint working between the two bodies, with close links at national and local levels, joint planning and interlocking targets for adults in learning; appropriate funding arrangements to support Ufl learning; and a co-ordinated approach to the establishment and accreditation of local learning centres in particular those with ICT-based provision.

Voluntary sector

4.27 The new arrangements will bring new opportunities for a wide variety of organisations currently involved in the planning and delivery of post-16 education and training, not least the voluntary sector. They are both the providers of specialist education and training and have a particular understanding of the needs of the disadvantaged and excluded people. The creation of a single Learning and Skills Council will simplify, and bring greater coherence to, arrangements for funding different types of education and qualifications, removing unnecessary bureaucracy and enabling the system to be more responsive to the needs of the individual. The voluntary sector's place in the new arrangements is an important one and will be funded under the same arrangements as colleges and other providers so long as they meet the essential quality and accountability thresholds that the Government is laying down. Voluntary organisations are particularly well placed to contribute their expertise in key areas such as tackling social exclusion and in the education and training of those with special or basic skill needs.

National Training Organisations

4.28 National Training Organisations (NTOs) have a pivotal role to play in the new arrangements. The Government attaches considerable importance to a strong sectoral approach as a means of better engaging employers and defining future skill needs. It will be essential to establish a clear and effective relationship between the new Council and the National Training Organisations and their representative body, the NTO National Council. As part of its remit the new Council should seek agreement with the NTOs on their workforce development plans and targets in England, and the NTO analysis of future learning and skill requirements should inform the strategy of the new Council. The Council should also have the capacity to invest in and deliver through the NTO network. The Government proposes to retain its sponsorship role in relation to employment sectors and the NTOs which serve them. NTOs have responsibilities across the whole UK, which include standard setting and the promotion of qualifications. The NTO network is still new and incomplete. The DfEE, working with administrations in Scotland, Wales and Northern Ireland and with Departments responsible for each employment sector, will ensure that the network is completed and strengthened, and ready to forge effective partnerships with the new Council, with RDAs and with the new Small Business Service.

> NTOs are new and influential, independent employment-led sector organisations recognised by the Department to work strategically with their sectors and with Government across education and training throughout the whole of the UK. They will help Government extend and improve its dialogue with employers to ensure that the needs of business are taken fully into account in developing policy.
>
> By the end of 1999 there will be more than 75 NTOs covering over 95% of the workforce.
>
> NTOs draw together wider employment interests including professional bodies, education, trades unions and trade associations. Their outputs include National Occupational Standards, Modern Apprenticeship and National Traineeship Frameworks.
>
> NTOs are required to provide sectoral labour market information - in future this will be according to a model called "Skills Foresight", which is used to influence training delivery, curriculum development and qualifications.

The Small Business Service

4.29 The Government has developed a new Small Business Service to offer help to a wide range of customers - from start-ups and micro-businesses to high-growth firms and those employing up to 250 employees. It will also provide help for those wishing to become self-employed and will encourage enterprise in deprived communities. For all these businesses, the focus of support will be aimed at removing barriers or providing assistance at each key stage of the firm's development. The Small Business Service will be the focus for improving the coherence of Government support and provide a single gateway for access to services directed primarily or mainly at small businesses. Local Learning and Skills Councils will need to work closely with the Small Business Service. In delivering workforce development services and programmes, for example, the local Learning and Skills Council will arrange with the SBS to provide a seamless service to business and to integrate skills development with enterprise and business competitiveness. The Government has issued a consultation document - 'The Small Business Service - a public consultation' (URM99/815) to seek views on the development of the service.

Higher Education

4.30 Higher education plays an important role in the education and training of our workforce - already one in three young people enter higher education. The Learning and Skills Council will need to take full account of the contribution and potential of this important sector and will work with the Higher Education Funding Council for England and with HE Institutions to achieve the National Learning Target for Level 4 (first degree or equivalent). Ensuring that there is seamless transition through learning so that everyone is able to progress to the highest level possible will be key. There is particular scope for collaborative activities and sharing facilities between universities and FE colleges, and for adult continuing education. We want to increase further the number of people who combine study with work, particularly in the 18-30 age group and at technician levels. We will be discussing these areas further with the higher education sector.

4.31 However, we do not propose that the Learning and Skills Council has direct funding responsibility for the higher education sector. This is for two reasons. First, uniquely, higher education's contribution is international and national as well as regional and local. Although universities should be responsive to the needs of local employers and business, both to meet skills requirements and in the application of research, they also operate on a wider stage and require a different approach to funding. Second, one of the main aims in creating the new Council is to bring order to an area which is overly complex, and where there are critical issues to address about coherence and the quality of provision. Including higher education would undermine this by complicating significantly the Council's remit and making that remit so broad as to be difficult to manage.

Investors in People (UK)

4.32 One of the core functions of the Learning and Skills Council will be to take forward the drive to achieve the national targets for organisations to be recognised as Investors in People. It will need therefore to work closely with Investors in People (UK) - see chapter 8.

Institutions and private training providers

4.33 Further education colleges are by far the largest providers of publicly funded post-16 education and training. There have been significant gains in the sector since 1993 in effective management, innovation in learning provision and in developing fruitful partnerships. Many colleges in their responses to recent consultations recognised the importance of strengthening partnerships and many are doing this. The proposals in this White Paper will build on FE strengths while ensuring that weaknesses are addressed robustly. We will encourage more FE colleges to engage further with other local partners in meeting the needs of their locality. The new Learning and Skills Council nationally and the local Councils will not succeed unless they establish strong and constructive relationships with local institutions and with the representatives of those institutions through their associations.

4.34 The TECs have also worked to improve the quality of private training providers. This is now being re-inforced by the work of the Training Standards Council. The arrangements for inspection and quality assurance set out in chapter 5 will be designed to continue these improvements. Private training providers will have an important place in the new arrangements and will be funded under the same arrangements for inspection and quality assurance as colleges so long as they meet the essential quality and accountability thresholds that the Government is laying down.

Question: How can we ensure that the Learning and Skills Council - and its local arms - develop effective links with its partners at national, regional and local level?

CHAPTER 5

Improving quality

5.1 At all stages of education and training, the central challenge is to improve the quality of learners' experiences. At present there are too many examples of weak provision, in particular:

- in the work-based route, there is too much poor practice among private training providers and others;

- in many sixth forms, especially smaller ones, there is substantial room for improvement; and

- in too many FE colleges there are significant curricular or managerial weaknesses.

5.2 Much current post-16 education and training is of good quality. To achieve our objectives, all provision must be consistently good and continuously improving. We must aim for the excellence which learners are entitled to expect from publicly funded education and training. We need a major drive to raise standards in post-16 provision as we have done in schools.

5.3 The Government has already made a start. In FE colleges and the work-based route, inspection reports and other performance information are used to identify good and poor practice and as the basis for raising standards. For the work-based route, the Government has strengthened the inspection arrangements and provided additional resources to address the programme of re-inspection. Training providers for their part are responding positively to the new culture of self-assessment and continuous improvement. In the FE sector the introduction of the FE Standards Fund, for which the Government has provided £115m from 1999-00 to 2000-01, is providing closely targeted expenditure to ensure weak colleges improve rapidly; to help the majority of colleges to raise their performance generally; and to reward excellent colleges by allowing them to spread their good practice. The general response from colleges has been strong enthusiasm for the Government's agenda, as their own plans for improvement are now being supported by this fund.

5.4 Quality improvement remains a critical part of our measures to improve the learning chances of students, particularly young people. These measures include better support, advice and guidance - see chapter 6. Better support will help to reduce drop out rates by guiding students to the right courses and helping them remain on them.

The aim

5.5 Everyone undertaking education and training should expect providers, whether they are FE colleges, sixth forms, private training providers or others to:

- demonstrate high and rising levels of retention, completion and achievement of learning objectives: it is unacceptable for performance to be as varied as it is.

- offer effective teaching and training by appropriately qualified staff who have opportunities for continuing training and development;

- provide a safe and supportive environment and respond speedily and effectively to the needs of every student;

- be well governed and managed; and

- deploy funds to achieve best value for money, and with the probity required of any body which receives public funding.

Supporting Quality Delivery

5.6   Post-16 quality assurance and inspection arrangements currently operate on a sectoral basis. These are described in appendix 3. Chapter 2 sets out how these distinctions mean that similar types of provision are inspected by different agencies according to their location, and how support for quality improvement varies as well.

5.7   The principal responsibility for quality improvement remains with providers themselves. The Government looks to all providers to adopt strategies for securing continuous improvement, as many do already. These strategies should be based on:

- self-assessment and action planning;

- obtaining and responding to the views of students and other customers about opportunities and services offered;

- setting in place effective mechanisms to receive, investigate and respond to concerns raised; and

- target setting using benchmarking based on relevant and consistent performance indicators.

5.8   Providers will be supported in two ways: by rigorous and independent external inspection, and by the Learning and Skills Council, which the Secretary of State will require to establish a quality improvement strategy, and a capacity for intervention to be applied in inverse proportion to success.

Inspection Arrangements

5.9   To ensure quality, independent rigorous inspection is vital. We intend to rationalise the existing inspection systems. Our aim is to provide a new coherence and unity in the inspection process for provision for young people through to the age of 19. We will also bring together the current arrangements for the inspection of provision for adults, and of work-based training, into a single new system.

5.10 OFSTED will be responsible for the inspection of provision for 16-19 year olds in schools and colleges. For post-19 provision in colleges, and for work-based provision for all age-groups, there will be a new independent Inspectorate. The two Inspectorates will work together, where appropriate, in the case of sixth form, tertiary and further education colleges. OFSTED will continue to inspect provision for the Youth Service. Adult and community education will be inspected by the new Inspectorate, as will appropriate provision within the ambit of the Ufl. The two Inspectorates will work together, where appropriate, to plan a joint inspection programme for sixth form, further education and tertiary colleges.

5.11 All inspections should be based on a common framework. The inspectorates must ensure that:

- inspections report on the quality of education and training provided, standards achieved, the supporting provider infrastructure, management, governance and value for money;

- the responsibilities of inspectors are clearly set out in relation to cross-college provision on the one hand, and curricular areas on the other; and

- a single reporting approach is adopted.

5.12 The Government will look to OFSTED to increase its focus on sixth form provision in schools. We wish to ensure that it is inspected in as much depth and as frequently as other school provision and 16-19 provision elsewhere. The Government will also look to OFSTED to lead area wide inspections for 16-19 education and training, encompassing all providers and in partnership with the new adult Inspectorate. These will focus on areas where the challenge to raise achievement and participation is particularly acute. Such inspections will not only make 16-19 providers more accountable by commenting on the match of provision to local demand, but will also support the Learning and Skills Council in its wider planning role.

5.13 In addition to carrying out their inspections of individual providers, both Inspectorates will:

- advise the Learning and Skills Council on the adequacy of action plans produced by providers to address weaknesses revealed in inspections, in return for funding to support improvement;

- monitor providers causing most concern on a continuing basis (including through formal re-inspections) until they can be moved out of that category or be subject to remedial action on the basis of continuing poor performance, as outlined above;

- prepare good practice reports drawn from inspection findings;

- undertake national surveys of key policy areas, and

- carry out international comparative studies.

The Learning and Skills Council: a quality improvement strategy

5.14 The Learning and Skills Council will be responsible for assuring itself of the quality of any body that it funds and agreeing a strategy for quality improvement generally with the Secretary of State. The Council will ensure that judgements about quality, standards and probity are part of its overall approach to funding and planning. Over time, the Council will move to a position where it only funds learning where providers effectively meet the expectations and fulfil the responsibilities described in paragraph 5.13 above. It will need to ensure that it has in place quality and audit systems which enable it to make accurate judgements about the performance of individual providers and elements of their programmes.

5.15 The Council will also be responsible for assuring the quality of provision to individuals and for ensuring that complaints are investigated promptly and thoroughly. It will not be enough for it to rely solely on external audit and inspection.

5.16 The Government will require the Council to reward high quality in education and training provision through both general and specific funding. It will work to ensure that this is celebrated, wherever it takes place. New arrangements for the education and training sector as a whole can build on those already in place to disseminate excellence in the FE sector, such as Beacon colleges.

5.17 The Government will expect the Council to take firm action where any provider is shown to fall short of the necessary standards of quality, support for students and probity. Except in cases of serious fraud, such providers should be given the opportunity to implement improvements. But where the response of providers is inadequate, the Secretary of State will look to the Council to propose remedial action.

5.18 In the case of Further Education colleges, where isolated examples of failure by a few can tarnish the good work of the many, Ministers announced new powers at the end of April for the Funding Council to appoint additional governors at college where it considers it appropriate, in addition to the existing powers of the Secretary of State for Education and Employment. Other options are a fresh start for a college under new management or merger. In the case of sixth forms, the local Learning and Skills Council would be able to make proposals relating to closure where inadequate progress had been made in securing the necessary improvements. The proposals would be considered by the School Organisation Committee and, if the Committee failed to agree, by the Schools Adjudicator, acting under guidance from the Secretary of State, as now. In the case of private training providers without similar corporate governance, the ultimate sanction would be withdrawal of Council funding.

5.19 The Learning and Skills Council will need to work closely with and, where necessary, support individual providers as they seek to implement improvements. More generally, to support its overall quality improvement strategy, the Council will:

- undertake research on quality issues of a long term rather than short term nature;
- advise the Secretary of State on the development of policies, and support their implementation;
- provide guidance on and promote staff training and development;
- promote best practice in education and training, including working with NTOs to secure improvements in work-based training;
- promote quality improvement through dissemination activity including publications and conferences etc; and
- monitor the numbers and types of complaints received to provide early warning of emerging issues and to ensure people receive the high quality service they have the right to expect.

5.20 In one area in particular, the Government itself will take the lead. Building on the work of the Further Education National Training Organisation (which sets the standards for FE college lecturers) and Employment National Training Organisations (which sets standards for work-based training and development, including private sector training providers) it will lead the development of a range of qualifications for all post-16 teaching and training staff. New requirements will be introduced as to the level of qualification which different categories of staff should obtain and the time which this should take. Where appropriate, we will seek consistency between the standards set for FE colleges and for work-based training, to strengthen the ethos of professionalism and parity of esteem between the different routes to learning. The Government will consult separately about the nature of the new requirements.

5.21 The Government will discuss with the Further Education Department Agency (FEDA), the National Training Organisations and other partners the most effective national arrangements for complementing and supporting the work of the Learning and Skills Council and the new arrangements for inspection, particularly in the area of developing, promoting, providing and offering guidance on staff training and development.

Question: *What more should we do to ensure we drive up quality in post-16 provision?*

Developing the Qualifications System

5.22 Qualifications are a measure of success for both individuals and providers. They are the currency by which individuals achieve progression within education and employment.   It is essential therefore that we have a rigorous and transparent system so that institutions and employers have confidence in the qualifications offered and can easily see how different levels and types of qualifications link together.

5.23 At present there is a confusingly large number of qualifications on offer. Public choice and confidence will be helped if these are rationalised and better quality assured. We have already asked the Qualifications and Curriculum Authority (QCA) to give these tasks the highest priority and we expect to endorse within a matter of weeks new criteria to apply to qualifications below degree level.

5.24 But this is not all that is required. We must ensure that young people attain a firm foundation of skills and knowledge across a broad range of study and that all are given defined challenges to meet. Earlier this year in the light of our *Qualifying for Success* consultation we announced important changes to the qualifications system to reflect our goals for young people. The changes were particularly designed to increase the range of choice available to young people so that they can follow the learning pathway best suited to their aspirations and abilities. In this context, we welcome the FEFC's intention to consult on proposals in support of our *Qualifying for Success* policies.

5.25 Key amongst the *Qualifying for Success* changes were:

- a new AS level to encourage take-up of more subjects in addition to the usual A levels;

- world class tests within the A level system to stretch the most able;

- linear and modular A level courses in all subjects with strict limits on coursework and an insistence on synoptic tests at the end of all courses;

- upgraded and more flexible GNVQs to enable more students to pursue a mix of academic and vocational subjects post 16; and

- a new key skills qualification to encourage all young people to continue to enhance their skills in communication, information technology and the application of number after the age of sixteen.

5.26 We are also asking the QCA to take forward the Skills Task Force proposal that, alongside NVQs studied 'on-the-job', young people on work-based training should undertake taught vocational qualifications covering the theory of their occupational area. This will open new opportunities for breadth and progression, and also mean a rationalisation of the enormous range of existing unregulated vocational qualifications. We are confident that these reforms will result in young people and colleges pursuing broader and more demanding programmes of work.

5.27 The needs of adults are different. They are more likely to be motivated by being able to take small steps towards a qualification, and some will want to take units from different qualifications. The QCA is rationalising NVQs and will ensure, with National Training Organisations, that they are based on standards which reflect the modern requirements of industry, while having a structure which allows more flexibility to better suit the operations of individual firms. The QCA's new criteria will also mean that college based vocational qualifications will consist of units based on occupational standards in a structured manner, so that they bear a clear relation to NVQs. We will ask the Learning and Skills Council to fund units of qualifications for adult learners. We support Sir Claus Moser's recommendations on qualifications for basic skills, and have commissioned the QCA to develop national standards of basic skill attainment to underpin qualifications and national tests.

5.28 Not all the activities of the Learning and Skills Council will be driven by qualifications. In particular, the new arrangements will mean that the awkward and artificial distinction of the 1992 Further and Higher Education Act, between qualifications covered by Schedule 2 and those outside it will no longer be needed. This will allow local Learning Partnerships to develop broader learning programmes covering, for example, basic skills, local history and vocational skills without needing to turn to different sources of funding for each. However, although not all the learning funded by the Council will lead to qualifications, we would expect it to give priority to courses that lead to nationally recognised qualifications and - more generally - to encourage learning towards recognised qualifications.

CHAPTER 6

Education and training of young people

6.1 Young people deserve the chance to be better qualified and to have the best possible start to their working lives. However, too many young people stop learning at 16. Indeed, some effectively stop learning well before then. This significantly affects their chances of making a success of their lives. Over 160,000 young people between 16 and 18 - around one in 11 of the age group - are not in learning nor in work; a proportion which has remained virtually unchanged since 1994. Only 74% of 19 year olds achieve level 2 qualifications and current levels of drop out from courses are too high.

6.2 Once young people become disengaged from learning or employment, they often face a number of problems such as offending, drug addiction and financial problems, which make their return progressively more difficult, and reinforce the need for high quality support and guidance. 63% of young offenders (mainly 15-20 year olds) are at or below NVQ level 1 in reading.

6.3 Young people can be 'turned off' education and training by poor experiences at any stage in their lives, but critical points usually occur between the ages of 13-19. This chapter describes a range of services and proposals designed to raise the number of young people continuing in education and training beyond 16; to reduce the levels of post-16 drop out by improving the quality of provision and of advice, guidance and support services; and to increase levels of attainment by driving up standards across all post-16 education and training in further education, work based learning and school sixth forms.

Our strategy for education and training for young people

6.4 Our strategy builds on the foundations we have laid through the wide ranging proposals for driving forward higher standards in our *Excellence in Schools* White Paper. These changes will lead to significant improvements in the qualification levels of young people up to the age of 16.

6.5 Our aspirations for young people post-16 are simple:

- to increase participation so that all young people can continue in education or training, including part-time study, until the age of 19. This will help them to make a good start on the ladder of lifelong learning - it will begin to equip them with the skills the workforce of the future needs, and it will prepare them to play an active role as good citizens;

- to improve attainment across all learning routes so that all young people are able to reach their full potential. We have set clear targets in relation to this for 2002.

6.6   We have done much during recent years, working through the Careers Service and others, to improve the quality of advice and guidance available to young people. And there are many examples of good practice by the Careers and Youth Services, educational and training providers and others. These have shown that innovative approaches and imaginative provision can successfully re-engage young people in learning and increase their chances of making a successful transition to adulthood. But if we are to succeed and make further progress, we must tackle the fragmented nature and variable quality of advice, guidance and support available to young people and the variable quality and relevance of some post-16 education and training. We must address the unacceptable position where too many people fail at school, where on average one in five courses taken by young people in further education colleges are not completed, and where as many as half of those in Government funded training leave their programmes early.

6.7   We will shortly announce an enhanced strategy - called *Connexions* - for making sure that far more young people continue in education and training until they are at least 19. This will build on current initiatives including:

- ensuring young people have the help, support and guidance that will raise their aspirations and tackle any personal and family problems standing in the way. We will make this support continuous from age 13-19 - through dedicated personal advisers, building on the Learning Mentors we announced in *Excellence in Cities*. For some, that will mean reaching out and bringing them back into learning. To do this, we will be introducing progressively from September 1999, a Learning Gateway for 16 and 17 year olds who need extra guidance and support to benefit from mainstream learning. Central to this will be the development of a network of personal advisers;

- encouraging employees aged 16-17, who did not achieve good qualifications at school, to take advantage of the new right to study or train for approved qualifications, with the support of their employer, so that they may take their place in the workforce of the future. Over half the 16-17 year olds not staying on in learning are in jobs without training;

- ensuring that the range of qualifications and courses is attractive and motivating, both to individuals and to employers. This will include broadening the options that are available at the age of 14, including the new GNVQ Part One, as well as a new qualification aimed at developing key skills in number, communication and information technology for all young people in their transition to adult life;

- building on the best work being done in schools, in colleges and in work based training to drive up quality and standards of delivery across all modes of learning; and

- tackling barriers to learning, including financial barriers. We have just introduced the first significant increase in minimum training allowances for over a decade and are taking significant steps to improve the current financial support available to FE and school sixth form students. As a first step we will be piloting Education Maintenance Allowances from September in 15 LEAs. These pilots will target financial support on young people from low income families who might otherwise be excluded. The results of this pilot will help inform new national arrangements for financial support. We are also considering ways in which we can target more specific help on the most disadvantaged where financial obstacles act as a real barrier to participation.

6.8 Increasing the number of young people who want to learn - and improving their success in getting skills and qualifications - will make the difference for individuals between a lifetime of low skills and low wages, and making a real contribution to society and gaining proper reward for it. All young people need access to high quality, comprehensive and impartial careers information, advice and guidance.

A new support service for young people

6.9 Our goal is to provide consistent and co-ordinated support for all young people when and where they need it, to enable everyone to stay on in learning - in a form and environment appropriate to them. Building on the Learning Gateway and our *Excellence in Cities* initiative in schools, **we intend to create new arrangements for providing support to young people**. The detail will be set out in the Social Exclusion Unit's (SEU) forthcoming report on 16-18 year olds not in education, training and work. The work the Department for Education and Employment and the SEU have done reveals very clearly that young people need differing levels of support and guidance, depending on their particular circumstances, if they are to make sensible and sustainable choices. They need information on the careers opportunities available. Support must be more accessible, both in terms of timing and location, and must be more personalised to the young person's individual needs.

6.10 The key aims of the new service will be to create a comprehensive structure for advice and support for all young people beyond 13, improving the coherence of what is currently provided through organisations such as the Careers Service, parts of the Youth Service and a range of other specialist agencies. The new service will represent a step change in the way this support is provided to young people, ensuring a smooth transition from compulsory schooling to post-16 options. It will integrate the present range of services and will provide high quality advice, guidance and support to all young people, wherever they live. The service will need to be flexible and outward looking so that it can respond to young people's particular needs. And it will be important that it is accessible to all. This means that it should be available to all young people at times, in places and in ways which meet their needs, rather than being driven by bureaucratic structures. This will require more outreach work, more imaginative ways of providing services and more joint working.

6.11 The new service will need to ensure coherence across current service boundaries, so that someone has an overview of the whole of a young person's needs - their education and training needs, and other needs which if not dealt with are likely to get in the way of education and training. Through the development of a comprehensive record system, it will ensure that prompt, co-ordinated action is taken if a young person stops being involved in education or training and risks 'dropping out'.

6.12 Making links with the range of voluntary activities, such as Millennium Volunteers, which young people choose to be involved in will be important too. As with Millennium Volunteers, young people will need to be involved in determining what should be provided through the new service. These opportunities can offer people the chance to develop personally and contribute directly to the re-building of local communities.

6.13 The responsibilities of the new service will extend to all 13-19 year olds, but it will particularly focus on keeping track of the most disadvantaged young people and helping those at most risk of dropping out - before and after the compulsory school leaving age - to remain in learning. It will seek to ensure that barriers to their learning are removed, and that they receive good and consistent advice and support centered on their individual needs, so that they can make the right choices to enable them to move into and stay in learning. In carrying out this function, however, it will be important that the service works with schools and colleges to make available appropriate provision to ensure that those young people who now stay on in learning continue to do so.

6.14 It will be important that the new service provides all young people with access to high quality, comprehensive and impartial careers information and advice, and that they are aware of both national and local labour market information to support their choices. This is an area which has been weak. The new service will need to adopt more imaginative approaches - and more innovative presentation of information making use of new and emerging technology - if it is to support all young people during their transition and also re-engage successfully those who are at risk of dropping out of learning.

6.15 The new service will need an innovative, effective and consistent means of local delivery, building on best current practice and substantially improving coverage and achievement. The service will be organised on the same geographical areas as the local arms of the Learning and Skills Council. The Government proposes to contract with bodies locally to provide the service in each area. Though this is a new service with a new vision, the Government's expectation is that the best careers service companies will play a major role, together with a range of other local partners. This will include working with the local Learning Partnerships on developing strategies to ensure the support meets the needs of young people at local level and that provision for young people is coherent with information, advice and guidance services for adults - see chapter 7. It will also need to work closely with the Employment Service which will continue to have responsibility, as now, for job broking services for 18 to 19 year olds who have joined the labour market, and for New Deal for 18-24 year olds. The Government intends to consult over the coming months on the detailed arrangements for the new service, including the extent to which it would include services currently provided by local authorities through the Youth Service and the Education Welfare Service.

Improving 16-19 provision

6.16 We believe that it is essential to co-ordinate the planning of all 16-19 provision in schools and colleges in order to raise standards and improve the opportunities available for young people beyond 16.

6.17 Measures introduced since 1997, including the resources made available through the Schools Standards and the FE Standards Funds, build on existing best practice in both the schools and FE sectors to reward achievement and tackle poor performance. The next three years will see £19 billion of extra investment spent on education. Within this an extra £725 million has been made available to FE over the two years 1999-2001 to widen participation and raise standards. Successful schools and colleges have become Beacons of Excellence. We must ensure that there are more of these each year across the country. The arrangements set out in this White Paper are intended to achieve this.

6.18 Standards are therefore at the heart of the Government's education agenda and any changes to the planning and funding arrangements will be designed to secure higher levels of achievement. For many young people in sixth forms, higher achievement means better A levels.

6.19 The total average points score achieved by 17 year old candidates attempting at least one GCE A level or AS equivalent is slightly higher in maintained schools (at 17.2 points, just under grades CCC at A level) than at FE colleges (at 14.8 points, just over CDD) who have a broader mix of students. In general, A/AS level outcomes are lower in maintained schools with smaller sixth forms, and in general FE colleges, with the following range: 10.8 in sixth forms with 50 or fewer pupils, and 18.6 in those with over 200; 17.2 in sixth form colleges, 14.2 in tertiary colleges and 9.0 in general FE colleges. But in all these cases, the distribution of marks within each sector is much wider than the difference between sectors. This means that there is at least as much work to do to raise performance within each sector as there is to address varying standards across sectoral boundaries.

6.20 We must ensure that poor performance is addressed as part of our drive to improve standards for all. We need to build in more transparency, so that parents can make more informed choices about their child's education and so that school governors can more easily assess the cost of running school sixth forms. We must ensure that we get value for money; greater transparency in funding will help achieve this. However, we share concerns that changes to the funding arrangements for school sixth forms must not be bureaucratic or a distraction for schools from the key task of raising standards.

6.21 The Government believes the following principles should govern any changes to 16-19 provision:

- the objective must be to improve overall standards of provision and tackle poor performing institutions;

- there should be no disruption for high quality sixth forms or colleges, but weaker sixth forms and colleges should be tackled, for instance by drawing them more fully into the pattern of local provision, increasing overall participation rates and standards;

- young people should be able to gain access to a broad learning programme, including A levels and vocational qualifications, wherever they are enrolled;

- improved co-ordination should ensure the best use of physical resources and the scarce expertise in a system, which should put the user, rather than competition between providers, at its heart;

- funding arrangements should be entirely transparent, taking account of the views of all interested parties; and

- LEAs should continue to have a key role in planning local secondary school education.

6.22 In the light of these principles, the Government proposes the following arrangements for changes to current arrangements for school sixth forms. Collaborative **planning** is essential to the successful co-ordination of post-16 provision, underpinned by the ability to intervene following inspection, as described in Chapter 5. The local Learning and Skills Council will therefore consult all local interests and have regard to guidance from the Secretary of State before drawing up a statement of priorities for 16-19 provision to reflect local needs. LEAs will consider these priorities when preparing their School Organisation Plans, as will School Organisation Committees (comprising key local partners in education) and Schools Adjudicators when considering LEAs' draft plans. The emphasis will be on collaboration throughout. The strengths of each provider will be built on; successful and popular 16-19 institutions, including schools, will be encouraged to expand; and collaboration between schools and other providers across the 14-19 curriculum will help increase standards and opportunities for all young people. Co-ordinated 16-19 planning will take account of the Government's commitment to reinforcing educational continuity for young people and removing unnecessary structural barriers to effective collaboration. Planning will also take account of local differences - for example, in relation to public transport links.

6.23 With regard to **funding**, many suggested in the consultation that the funding for school sixth forms should be brought together with other funding for 16-19 year olds to create a single post-16 budget. They argued that this would allow funding to follow individual choices more easily and would promote and facilitate collaboration between schools and colleges.

6.24 A number of LEAs, notably East Sussex and Lewisham, are already piloting, in collaboration with local schools, alternative funding models for school sixth forms within the Fair Funding framework. The pilots have explored the benefits of allocating funding more effectively and fairly among the school sixth forms within an LEA to reinforce good practice within schools to raise standards and performance. The report into the pilots, published in October 1998, concluded that they had highlighted the ways in which school sixth form funding could and should be more closely matched to the needs and requirements of students and schools, and that they therefore had the potential to contribute to raising standards in school sixth forms. The most effective results from the new funding approaches came from the use of transparent and clear principles, that are easily understood by individual schools in the calculation of their budget. A number of other LEAs are now following East Sussex's lead.

6.25 The Government has decided to bring the funding of 16-19 provision in colleges and in work based training within the remit of the new Council, and can see attractions in doing so for LEA sixth form provision too. Its view is that further consideration is needed on this issue. *School Sixth Form Funding: a consultation paper* (Ref: P16LRCD) is published today. This emphasises that there is no question of levelling down sixth form funding or imposing unnecessary bureaucratic burdens. Copies can be ordered from the Department for Education and Employment's Publications Centre, Sherwood Park, Annesley, Nottingham, NG1S 0DJ; tel: 0845 60 222 60; fax: 0845 60 333 60. The paper is also on the Internet at http://www.dfee.gov.uk/sixthform.

6.26 All responses should be sent to:
Gerald Staines
Department for Education and Employment
Funding and Organisation Division
Sanctuary Buildings
Great Smith Street
London SW1P 3BT

or by e-mail to: **sixthform.response@dfee.gov.uk**

CHAPTER 7

Supporting adult learners

7.1   All adults need the opportunity to continue to learn throughout their working life, to bring their qualifications up to date and, where necessary, to train for a different job. Now and in the future, employability is and will be the best guarantee of employment. Learning also brings broader benefits. It encourages and supports active citizenship, helps communities help themselves, and opens up new opportunities such as the chance to explore art, music and literature. It helps strengthen families and encourages independence. That means that everyone must have access to high quality, relevant learning at a time and pace, and in places that suit them. Not only do individuals, families and communities benefit, learning throughout life also delivers tangible results for business - improved productivity and competitiveness.

7.2   Much needs to be done to achieve our vision. Seven million adults have no formal qualifications at all and the number of jobs requiring low level skills is declining. 55% of the adult population does not have a level 3 qualification.

7.3   In this country we have a significant problem with the level of basic skills among adults - over one in five have real problems with literacy and numeracy. This places us well behind many of our competitors - ninth out of 12 countries covered in an OECD study. While this is partly the legacy of many years of under achievement in schools, it also results from the inadequacies of current opportunities for adult learning. In relation to basic skills, and more generally, there has been insufficient demand. Too few adults want to learn and supply has not always been organised around the needs ˙ and motivations of potential adult learners.

7.4   Although there are many individual examples of excellence, the fragmentation of the system has meant that no one has had the incentive or the power to put this right across the country as a whole. Our reforms will address this problem. As chapter 2 and the rest of this chapter set out, we have put in place a major programme of work and significant additional resources to begin to address this. We are stimulating demand, especially through individual learning accounts and the Ufl and through promoting the benefits of learning in partnership with broadcasters and others. We are modernising supply through Ufl IT learning centres and through changes in the organisation of FE colleges and community provision. The creation of a single Council covering all forms of (non higher education) adult learning will mean that for the first time one organisation will be responsible for delivering services to this group and meeting the Government's Targets.

7.5   We expect the new Council to work with others to champion lifelong learning, promoting learning to men and women of all ages, including older people as well as returners to the labour market and those with special needs. Older people, for example, benefit greatly from learning. Research has shown that older people who continue to be active learners enjoy healthier lifestyles and maintain their independence longer than those who stop learning. Grandparents can also play an important role in family learning, supporting children to acquire good reading skills. The Learning and Skills Council will work to break down barriers to older people playing a full part in a learning society.

7.6 The Council, working with the Ufl, will build on the start FE colleges, TECs, local authorities, private and voluntary providers have made:

- using new technologies to promote open and distance learning; and

- making provision more flexible, accessible and responsive; for example by offering learning at the weekend, in holiday periods and in the evenings or delivering in the community often in partnership with community and voluntary sector organisations and relating directly to community needs.

Demand for learning

7.7 The new Council will have a clear role to play in driving up demand for learning so as to complement the impact of individual learning accounts and the Ufl, and support the work of NIACE, the Campaign for Learning and broadcasters in promoting learning throughout life. To deliver its objectives the Learning and Skills Council, and those organisations it funds, will work with broadcasters, the media, the Ufl and others in the private and voluntary sector to promote the value of learning to people and the benefit it can bring to their lives.

Individual Learning Accounts

7.8 Individual learning accounts are a major strand in the Government's programme for a lifelong learning revolution. In February 1998, we set out the aims for individual learning accounts in the Green Paper *The Learning Age* and in *Opportunity Scotland*. Individual learning accounts will be a key addition to the package of support available to learners, and for the first time people will have a mechanism to help them plan and manage their own learning. People will invest their own money in their account, but the responsibility is not with the individual alone. We are seeking to provide a vehicle for funding continuous learning where the Government, employers and the individual can all have a part to play.

7.9 The Government has already announced a substantial package of incentives for individual learning accounts. The incentives are:

- for the first million starter accounts, a contribution of £150 for each individual in the first year of the account, subject to a small contribution from them;

- a 20% discount off the cost of eligible courses on spending up to £500 in each year (this applies from the second year of an account, if the individual has a starter account);

- an 80% discount off the cost of certain other courses, including computer literacy;

- employees will not be subject to tax or National Insurance Contributions on any employer's contribution to a learning account for eligible learning, as long as the employer extends the facility to the lowest paid employees in the company on a similar basis; and

- contributions made by employers will be tax deductible.

7.10 UK employers already invest over £10 billion each year in training and development. It is the employer's responsibility to invest in the skills of their employees to meet business objectives. Individual learning accounts should add to this and offer scope for joint investment in development which will directly benefit both the individual and the employer through increased motivation and better staff morale.

7.11 Individual learning accounts will be a key addition to the package of support available to learners. Unemployed people are offered support with learning and skills development through the New Deals and related programmes. Individual learning accounts will be aimed towards people in work or those about to enter work to help them fulfil their potential for independence and self-investment.

7.12 We hope that financial institutions will play a major part in setting up and running individual learning accounts. The new Learning and Skills Council will have an important role to play in promoting and marketing them against the clear national framework and a supporting administrative system which the Government will be setting up. This is described in more detail in *Individual Learning Accounts - A Summary of Progress* published in May 1999.

Ufl

7.13 The Ufl is a major plank in the Government's programme to deliver a learning society. It will provide adult learners with greater choice and flexibility by stimulating innovative modes of provision and delivery which are responsive to people's needs and circumstances. To be launched nationally in autumn 2000, the Ufl will promote lifelong learning and will work with a wide range of partners to provide flexible access to high quality, relevant innovative learning opportunities. It will offer a free, comprehensive information and advice service and will broker a national learning network with learning materials which will allow people to learn at home, in the workplace or in learning centres based in their communities. The Ufl's plans are described in *A New Way of Learning: The Ufl Network - Developing the University for Industry Concept* published in March 1999 (available on www.ufiltd.co.uk).

7.14 The new Learning and Skills Council will work closely with the Ufl to improve the overall coherence and responsiveness of education and training provision for adults and help embed lifelong learning in people's daily lives.

Promoting adult learning

7.15 What can be achieved is clearly shown through the recent *Brookie basics* campaign. Through the medium of Channel 4's soap *Brookside* many thousands of people have been linked with local opportunities to improve their literacy. The BBC's *Computers Don't Bite* and *Webwise* campaigns also gave thousands the chance to use computers and explore the Internet for the first time. Every year Adult Learners' Week, organised through NIACE, celebrates and promotes adult learning acting as a focus for hundreds of events up and down the country. Positive messages about learning are sent to people with their Benefit Giros. Partnership with broadcasters and Learning Direct provides information about learning opportunities to thousands of people.

7.16 The development of digital broadcasting, and the establishment of dedicated learning channels and related on-line services - such as *BBC Knowledge* - will offer further opportunities to promote and engage a wide range of people in learning in their homes and elsewhere.

7.17 We will expect the Council to develop a clear strategy to promote adult learning in these and in other innovative ways.

Supporting adults through good quality information, advice and guidance services

7.18 We want to make sure that adults have the help they need to make informed choices about learning. According to the National Adult Learning Survey, one in five adults know little about the kind of learning opportunities that are available locally. One in ten say they want to learn, but cannot find what they are looking for where they live. Others, particularly the socially disadvantaged or those who otherwise lack confidence, often need a good deal of support and encouragement before they can take the first few steps back into learning. Moreover, wider changes mean that the demand for good quality information and advice will increase over the next few years. In particular, changes in the labour market mean that individuals can expect to change their job much more frequently. And as a result of the policies set out in this White Paper, the number of adults seeking learning - and therefore in need of help in thinking through the kind of learning that is best for them - will rise significantly.

7.19 For all of these reasons, there is a good case for improving the quality and coverage of the services which provide adults with information, advice and guidance about learning. Historically, there has been no statutory or other requirement on any agency to deliver these services and they have developed largely in response to local initiatives. Although there are excellent services in some parts of the country, they are not yet in place everywhere.

7.20 Against this background, we have already taken a number of steps to improve information, advice and guidance services. In particular, starting this year, we have introduced a new national £54 million programme to deliver an information and advice service for adults at local level. The programme has a clear emphasis on giving adults the kind of practical help that they need. Once local services are fully established, they will ensure that in every part of the country, adults can access comprehensive information about the learning opportunities available in their areas. And they will be able to talk through the possibilities - and what they might do about them - with a qualified adviser.

7.21 The programme is being supported through the local Learning Partnerships and will be delivered by a wide variety of local organisations, including local authorities, careers services and voluntary and community bodies which are often closest to local people. Each local Learning Partnership will produce a plan showing how the different players will work together to meet local needs. These arrangements will have a particular emphasis on helping the socially disadvantaged and disabled people, for whom information, advice and guidance can have such an important role.

7.22 In addition, we have set up Learning Direct, the first national helpline which provides information and advice about learning. The service has helped over 700,000 callers since it was launched in February 1998. Under the management of Ufl, Learning Direct's services will continue be developed and extended so that it can handle up to 1.5 million calls annually by 2002.

7.23 Learning Direct will complement and reinforce on a national level the services that are being developed locally, for which it will act as an important entry point. For example, callers to Learning Direct who need advice that can only be informed by a local perspective, will be referred to their local information and advice service; similarly, local services will also need to refer some enquiries to Learning Direct. The general intention is that from the point of view of the learner there should be a seamless service. Finally, Personal Advisers are providing a more comprehensive advice and support service through the Gateway associated with New Deal that is aimed specifically at young people, the long-term unemployed and people with disabilities.

7.24 All of these developments are very new. The structural changes outlined elsewhere in this White Paper nevertheless provide an opportunity to take them a step further. To ensure that they are properly integrated with mainstream learning provision, **responsibility for planning and funding adult information, advice and guidance services will transfer to the Learning and Skills Council from April 2001**. Locating the responsibility with the body tasked with overseeing the great majority of post-16 learning will also help to ensure that information, advice and guidance services remain at the heart of the development of public policy rather than - as has sometimes been the case in the past - on the margins.

Supply of learning opportunities

7.25 To improve the supply of learning opportunities, the Council will build on existing examples of excellence. It will work with the Ufl and others so that people have information, advice and guidance about, and easy access to, learning that meets their requirements and circumstances. We will achieve this in the following ways:

IT Learning Centres

7.26 The March Budget announced Capital Modernisation Fund provision to establish some 700 IT learning centres for adults and businesses to improve access to technology and ICT-based learning in communities, especially disadvantaged areas. These centres, which will be developed over the next three years, are expected to engage a wide range of partners from the public, private and voluntary sectors. The Government is putting in place structures to ensure effective co-ordination with other relevant initiatives, in particular the Ufl network, to increase the impact locally in communities.

Further Education

7.27 Three million adults are already learning, usually part-time, in FE colleges. Further education gives many the first chance to learn since leaving school. Many other people learn in other settings, including within the voluntary sector. The number will increase by 20% over the next three years. New funding arrangements have been introduced to support colleges and their partners in reaching out to people who have not traditionally taken part in learning. These have helped in some cases to provide opportuities in community settings or by using ICT and in other cases helped people to get to classes easily by working with transport service providers. The Ufl will play an important part in supporting colleges in this.

7.28 The range and quality of opportunities available are being extended and improved through the initiatives we have introduced. The FE sector is also taking action to ensure that its provision meets the needs of people with disabilities. Our proposals in this respect are described in Chapter 4.

7.29 The Learning and Skills Council will build on all these developments, developing a truly comprehensive approach to adult learning.

Learning in the community

7.30 Adult and community based learning form a vital part of the Government's drive to widen participation in learning, to build communities' self-confidence and capacity, and to promote good citizenship and regeneration. They embrace a wide variety of learning environments - pubs, clubs, community and leisure centres, health centres, as well as opportunities provided or arranged by local authorities in adult education institutions or schools or by voluntary organisations. They can address the specific needs of particular communities and groups, and thus can be focused on key local issues such as crime prevention or housing. Such opportunities are often a way of enabling adults to get back to the starting line for learning to gain in confidence as well as acquire skills. They can also support family learning and have a particular role to play in tackling the nation's legacy of poor basic skills which has been identified in the recent Moser report, *Improving Literacy and Numeracy - a Fresh Start.*

7.31 Local authorities currently have a duty to secure the provision for their area of those aspects of further education which fall outside the remit of the Further Education Funding Council. Essentially this is for adult and community learning that does not lead to formal national qualifications, or otherwise meet the criteria for funding by the FEFC. The main source of direct funding for adult and community learning has been through local authority block grant. Local authorities are free to spend this as they see fit in the light of their needs and circumstances. Their current direct spending in this area amounts to some £120 million, about half what it was five years ago. But this spending varies enormously, ranging from 50 pence per head in some places to £25 - fifty times as much - in others .

7.32 Other resources have been an increasingly important contributor to adult and community education in recent years: notably the Single Regeneration Budget, European Structural Funds, resources from other local authority budgets, such as libraries or leisure services and the National Lottery. Museums, art galleries and heritage sites increasingly offer adults as well as children new and exciting ways to engage in learning that enhances the spread of our rich cultural inheritance.

7.33 Despite this rich variety of opportunities, provision is increasingly patchy. In some parts of the country men and women of all ages - including older people - do not have access to the range and breadth of opportunities that interest them. Lack of opportunity leads to poverty of aspiration in a self-reinforcing cycle of decline. As well as improving the range and quality of provision we must find new ways of re-motivating and re-engaging those who have few, if any, qualifications.

7.34 This will also be essential if we are to build the learning communities we wish to see. The Government has already taken steps to re-invigorate adult and community learning by introducing Standards Fund support for local education authorities, by establishing family literacy and numeracy initiatives and by launching an Adult and Community Learning Fund.

7.35 The establishment of the new Learning and Skills Council provides an opportunity to build on this progress and integrate adult and community learning more effectively with other types of provision. The Government therefore proposes to introduce legislation that would:

- give the new Council the national duty to arrange adequate and sufficient adult and community learning provision; and

- give to local authorities the changed duty to contribute to arrangements for provision at local level.

7.36 Reflecting these changes directly, the Government would propose to:

- move from local authority block grant to the Learning and Skills Council the element of expenditure related to adult education; and

- direct the Learning and Skills Council, through its local arms, to arrange provision in the light of plans drawn up by local Learning Partnerships to which local authorities would make a key contribution in pursuance of their duty as described above.

7.37 Under these arrangements local authorities would be required as now to prepare lifelong learning plans which local Learning Partnerships would take into account in proposing programmes to meet the identified local needs of their communities. Providing these requirements are met effectively, the Council would have the clear objective to ensure that a substantial part of the available resource is directed to provision arranged by local authorities. Local authorities will therefore continue to have a key role in this important area, and in particular will have the opportunity to ensure that this provision is delivered in ways which are well integrated with local authorities' other services and the wider needs of their areas. Local arms of the Learning and Skills Council would have considerable discretion in the level and type of funding for different types of learning opportunity which do not fit neatly within the new national tariff arrangements. They could also give local Learning Partnerships discretionary budgets to support activity in very local areas within their boundaries. We will consult further on the detailed arrangements.

7.38 In this way we intend to drive the growth of new opportunities bottom up. Locally connections will also be made with IT learning centres and the Ufl, as well as with college provision so that, over time, we will achieve greater consistency and breadth in the range and scale of opportunities available to all adults, wherever they live.

Basic skills

7.39 Our new arrangements will provide a much more coherent approach to encouraging and helping people improve their literacy and numeracy. The Council will be specifically required to ensure that such provision - whether in colleges, voluntary and community organisations, workplace or elsewhere - is given high priority in all local plans, is of high quality and is effectively resourced. Local Learning Partnerships will include in their adult and community plans specific provision for basic skills.

7.40 In this way we will build on the recommendations in the Moser report so that we make real inroads into reducing the legacy of poor skills that affects so many people and businesses.

Question: *In what further ways can the Learning and Skills Council deliver improvements in adult learning?*

Supporting unemployed people back to work through learning

7.41 Employers place a premium on recruiting people without long breaks in their work history, and who can demonstrate the skills needed in the workplace. Helping people who are out of work find and keep a job is therefore a priority for Government. Most people find work relatively quickly and the best and quickest route back to work will be through the job matching services of the Employment Service supported, where appropriate, by help with job search and advice. Some jobseekers, however, need training to boost their employability. This can range from developing basic skills to more occupationally specific learning. People who need this training must have both the motivation and the opportunity to train whether in the workplace or outside it.

7.42 Unemployed people and others not in employment, can upgrade their skills through three main ways:

- through access to further education without having to pay fees, and undertaking study of their own choice. Those who are claiming Jobseekers' Allowance (JSA) may not study, however, for more than 16 guided hours a week and they remain subject to the availability for work conditions of JSA. This is also the route available for those on New Deal for Lone Parents, New Deal for Partners of the Unemployed, and New Deal for People with Disabilities;

- people on New Deal for 18-24 year olds and those over 25 have access to further education and training on a full-time basis on the advice of Personal Advisers where this is thought the best way of overcoming barriers to re-entering the labour market. This is paid for under contract from the Employment Service from New Deal funds; and

- through TEC funded work based learning for adults, which provides basic and occupational skills training for unemployed people over the age of 25.

7.43 In addition, unemployed adults can benefit from adult and community learning opportunities funded by Local Education Authorities.

7.44 The Government has already greatly improved the opportunities that are available to unemployed people. The New Deal offers personal advice together with real skills and training opportunities to people who have too often been failed by the system in the past. But we need to do more. **The Government intends to simplify current arrangements by transferring responsibility for work based learning for adults from TECs to the Employment Service**. This will achieve a greater integration of the skills agenda with the Welfare to Work agenda and in particular the New Deal. The change will happen from April 2001, in line with the other major changes that will be implemented at that time.

7.45 These changes alone will produce a substantial improvement in the quality of service and range of opportunities that unemployed men and women will see and experience. There is, however, a case for going further and looking again at the way that unemployed people are supported and advised through spells of further education. Current rules, which permit study while claiming JSA under the 16 hour rule, are designed to offer flexibility to jobseekers to benefit from learning while ensuring that they maintain a strong attachment to the labour market and get a new job as soon as possible. There is, however, evidence that those studying under these arrangements do not always follow a course of study, or achieve learning goals, of a kind or at a speed to maximise their prospect of improving their long-term employability. Others have difficulty obtaining support for learning which would be of assistance to them. Front-line staff in the Employment Service do not always find it easy to resolve the inevitable tensions in the current arrangements between an individual's wish to complete their course of study and the requirement to be available for work.

7.46 One possible way ahead would be to introduce arrangements which give better advice to unemployed adults who choose to pursue further education, to ensure that taking up a particular opportunity will genuinely enhance their skills and employability. This could be done by, for example, ensuring that all those who studied under the 16 hour rule did so with the benefit of a personal action plan which would be agreed with their Employment Service Personal Adviser and which would set out how the additional skills would improve an individual's prospects in the labour market. This process of providing guidance and support is being rapidly developed through the ONE pilots, which integrate the Employment Service, Benefits Agency and local authority services to help people find jobs, and which were launched by the Government on 28 June.

7.47 There is also a case for examining whether it would be right to allow more people to undertake full time study or a positive programme of volunteering while unemployed in circumstances in which an immediate return to work is unlikely. This would be linked to the course of activity being one which, in the opinion of their Adviser, was likely substantially to improve their job prospects and could also be arranged with the payment of allowances in a similar way to work based learning and the New Deal for 18-24s. Further work will be done to bring greater coherence to the funding of education and training for unemployed people and to find the best way of ensuring that they have the right opportunities to gain new skills where it will help them get jobs. This work will build on evidence from New Deal and the thorough evaluation of the Jobseeker's Allowance. Lessons learned from the ONE pilots will also feed into this work.

7.48 It will be important that, in planning provision, the Employment Service and the Learning and Skills Council work closely together at national level to ensure that planning and funding systems are consistent and use common payment and audit arrangements whenever possible. Joint planning at a local level will also be necessary so that provision meets employer and individual needs and is planned to eliminate duplication and overlaps.

Question: *What more should we do to ensure we develop coherent provision for unemployed people to gain the skills they need and to tackle the other barriers they face in finding and keeping work?*

CHAPTER 8

Encouraging learning businesses

The benefits to business

8.1 The proposals set out in this White Paper offer business two important benefits. First, they will raise standards and skills. Second, they offer the opportunity to build better links with the wider education system and to use the information employers have on the skills they require to influence more effectively the types and nature of learning that institutions offer.

8.2 The fortunes of businesses and individuals in the modern economy are now inextricably linked. Individuals without the relevant skills and qualifications will find increasing difficulty in gaining and retaining good quality jobs. Businesses without a well motivated and skilled workforce will have increasing difficulty surviving. Leading edge employers encourage diversity in the background, skills and approach of their workforce.

8.3 The benefits to business of employees with higher skills are clear. Businesses with higher skills are able to adapt better to new technology and use it effectively. Product and service quality is higher, there is less waste from sub-standard production and productivity is higher. These are all characteristics of leading edge firms. The same pattern emerges from international benchmarking studies comparing similar firms in the same industries across national boundaries. Higher skills mean that businesses are less likely to encounter skill shortages at the peaks of the economic cycle. Employers who train are more effective in retaining good quality staff and in maintaining the commitment of their employees. Successful employers are those who realise that their people are their most important asset - and act on that by investing in their skills and development.

8.4 The actions of individual employers, especially the millions of small businesses, will have a major impact on the skills that individuals develop and on productivity in the economy. If we are to succeed, our reforms must lead to a significant increase in the proportion of employed people who undertake training and retraining, especially in the workplace, throughout their working lives. We are therefore determined that businesses should play a full part in the Learning and Skills Council at national and local level and use the new arrangements as a platform for action on the level of skills.

Engaging businesses

8.5 Employers have already made a valuable contribution to post-16 education and training through their involvement with colleges, TECs and local Learning Partnerships. The new Learning and Skills Council offers business at national and local levels the opportunity of engagement on the wider canvas whilst offering new opportunities through the Small Business Service. National Training Organisations, which are employer led bodies, will continue to play a pivotal role in the new system, as set out in chapter 4. The local Learning and Skills Councils will provide the key interface for engaging most employers. Working closely with the Small Business Service and the local Learning Partnerships, they will develop long term relationships with the majority of employers within their area.

8.6 Through involvement as members of the national and local Learning and Skills Councils, business people will have a direct opportunity to feed into the education system, their perspective, about how the world of work is changing and how the requirements for particular types of skills are developing in response to changes in technology and working practices. In addition to those business people who contribute their time as members of the local Learning and Skills Council, we expect the Council to ensure opportunities exist for the wider business community to contribute their views. Through their involvement locally, people will have the opportunity to influence skills and employability within their local labour force which can, over time, offer real business benefits. This engagement will be the key to bringing education and business more closely and productively together. It will be reinforced by the involvement of business led RDAs in assessing and monitoring local plans and advising the national Council (see chapter 4). Through this, education and training providers will have the information to enable them to adapt their learning programmes so that they are more up to date and in touch with business needs. They will also be better able to plan ahead and advise learners about the labour market and the career opportunities offered by different learning programmes. In addition, education and training providers will be able to see much more clearly how courses in institutions and training provided by employers can fit more effectively together.

Question: are the measures proposed sufficient to engage business in the new arrangements?

Role of the Learning and Skills Council

8.7 The Learning and Skills Council will be responsible for creating a clear national agenda for action on workforce development, working with employers, the Small Business Service, trade unions, National Training Organisations, trade associations, Investors in People UK and the UfI. To underpin this it will develop:

- a **clear framework** that enables everyone involved to recognise and understand relevant roles and responsibilities;

- **better signposting and links** between existing organisations and activities;

- **clear benchmarks for quality** of provision and a means of assessing it;

- truly **responsive and flexible provision**, facilitated (not hampered) by appropriate funding mechanisms;

- the ability to **target Government funding**, for maximum impact; and

- a strategy for working with employers to **promote the benefits to business of becoming a learning business**.

Action at national level

8.8 The Learning and Skills Council will provide the context both for the activities of other key national players and for local action and delivery. As a result decisions on workforce development can then be effectively joined up with decisions on other post-16 education and training provision. We propose that the new Council should at a national level:

- implement improved arrangements for collecting and disseminating labour market and skills information, building on the recommendations in the second report of the national Skills Task Force;

- prepare and publish a strategy for skills and workforce development;

- offer advice on appropriate National Learning Targets for workforce development and how those can be delivered; and

- identify best practice in establishing and meeting skill needs and disseminate this through the network of local Learning and Skills Councils.

8.9 The development of a better system of collecting and analysing labour market and skills information is an important new responsibility. This will build on the proposals in the second report of the Skills Task Force. The objective is to make information more consistent and coherent, more forward looking and focused directly on the people who need it. Better information will allow markets to work more effectively. As part of the new arrangements, the Learning and Skills Council will prepare and publish an annual skills assessment. Similar assessments will be prepared at local level. The national assessment will lead to the identification of key sectors where the national Council might stimulate action, in co-operation with relevant National Training Organisations, Regional Development Agencies and local Learning and Skills Councils. National Training Organisations will have a particular role in informing the Council about expected changes in technology, occupational structures and skills needs within their sectors. This will help ensure that the Learning and Skills Council's national plans are not simply extrapolations of past trends but are based on a strong dialogue with employers about changes affecting particular sectors and occupations.

8.10 The development of the UfI will reinforce the Learning and Skills Council's role on workforce development. The UfI's objectives include the stimulation of demand for lifelong learning among businesses, improved access to relevant, high quality learning opportunities and a learner-centred set of principles which will make it easier for people to learn in bite-sized units in the workplace at a time convenient to them and their employer.

8.11 The trade unions also have a vital role to play in workforce development. Effective investment in workforce development depends on joint investment, with individuals, employers and the Government all playing a part. Trade unions can make a real difference by working to add value to individual contributions so that the total impact on workforce development is more than the sum of the parts. Unions have already demonstrated how successfully they can make an impact through the innovative 'Bargaining for Skills Programme', which has given a new impetus to employers and their workforce to plan together to improve the opportunities that individuals have to acquire skills. The Union Learning Fund is playing a key part in developing a network of Learner Representatives which, together with a diverse range of initiatives designed to boost the quality, quantity and scope of learning in the workplace, is making a reality of lifelong learning for many more people. This excellent work serves to underpin one key emerging message: the role of the trade union is clearly important, but that role is changing. Their activity is increasingly focused on ensuring the long term employability of their members through innovative strategies for developing skills in the workplace. Under the new arrangements, the Learning and Skills Council will work closely with trade unions to ensure that this important role is encapsulated and continued.

8.12 It is important that investors, potential employees and the wider community should be aware of what employers do to invest in their people. The "People Skills Scoreboard" is a new approach, developed originally by the Engineering Employers Federation (EEF) and the Engineering and Marine Training Authority (EMTA). It is aimed at encouraging employers to declare their investment in training, and is now being further piloted jointly by the DfEE and the DTI. Employer participation in the Scoreboard is on a voluntary basis. We intend to extend this initiative into further sectors over the coming year; and will be looking at how we can build from this approach to ensure that the substantial investment that employers make in their people is more transparent through reporting arrangements. Subject to satisfactory evaluation, the Learning and Skills Council will then build the lessons into the action plans it generates at local level.

Relationship with Investors in People (UK)

8.13 Investors in People (UK) performs a key role in keeping the national standard for Investors in People up to date, maintaining its integrity and in national marketing and promotion to organisations. The Government is keen that this existing role should continue and that there should be strong links between the new Learning and Skills Council and Investors in People (UK). This will mean that the new Council will take responsibility for meeting the targets for Investors in People recognitions, along with other National Learning Targets. It will also be important for Investors in People (UK) to work effectively through the Small Business Service in engaging businesses.

National and multi-site companies

8.14 An important aspect of the work of the Learning and Skills Council at national level will be to build strong relationships with large national companies who find it difficult to work effectively within the current system. Despite the efforts made by TECs, the current approach to reconciling the needs of national companies within a locally driven system is bureaucratic, costly to run and ineffective. The Learning and Skills Council will be able to work directly with such employers to help identify their learning and skills needs and the contribution they can make to raising levels of attainment.

Action at local level

8.15 Local Learning and Skills Councils will draw up robust local strategies for skills within a national framework and with clearly assigned roles and responsibilities for all the key partners. Working, in particular, with Regional Development Agencies, and through the Small Business Service, local Learning and Skills Councils will provide a wide range of practical help to individual businesses, for example:

- support in developing effective training plans which match the skills of an employer's workforce to the current and future needs of the business;

- advice and support in the implementation of the Investors in People standard;

- targeted support for addressing critical skill needs and shortages especially for upskilling and retraining of key personnel; and

- help with the recruitment and training of new young employees through Modern Apprenticeships and National Traineeships, either through direct contracts or through an accredited preferred provider.

8.16 Local Learning and Skills Councils will also be the main vehicle for taking forward at local level the implementation of national skill priorities, e.g. the recommendations of the national Skills Task Force on IT and of regional priorities identified by the Regional Development Agencies. To do this effectively, local Learning and Skills Councils will take forward the work of TECs and others in developing strong local employer networks, often built around supply chains, in key sectors of the local economy. These sector-based networks will strengthen the role and influence of employers in the planning and quality of further education and training and articulate more effectively current and future skill needs. They will draw on the expertise of relevant National Training Organisations and will be central to the skills and workforce development strategies produced by the local Learning and Skills Councils. These strategies should include the regular publication of a local skills assessment, based on a thorough analysis of the provision and availability of skills and on up to date information on skill recruitment patterns. It will highlight key skill shortages and be linked to an action plan setting out how the local Learning and Skills Council is addressing these issues in its long term strategy and through direct immediate intervention.

8.17 Local Learning and Skills Councils will give support and encouragement to these sector networks to develop "preferred supplier arrangements" with colleges and other specialist training providers in their sector. This will strengthen the purchasing power of businesses in negotiating flexible and cost-effective provision that meets their needs. Local Learning and Skills Councils will also give practical help to employers to develop shared facilities for training by pooling specialist staff resources or helping to establish Group Training Associations; and will work with trade unions to integrate the approach of 'Bargaining for Skills' and other initiatives into their action plans.

8.18 Businesses also have a key role to play in stimulating demand for learning from individuals, in particular through individual learning accounts. Many employers are now recognising that employee development schemes (e.g. Peugeot Motor Company - see box below) which provide more broadly based career development for the individual, also benefit the employer through increased motivation and better retention of staff.

> Peugeot Motor Company runs a successful Employee Development Programme which arose from joint negotiations between trade unions and management. It is open to company emploees and offers financial support of up to £250 per year for them to develop new skills or improve basic/key skills. It reintroduces people to learning, many of whom have been out of education for many years. In the last finacial year, approximately 23% of Peugeot staff took up the opportunity to join the Assisted Development Programme, 24% taking a general interest subject, and 76% taking a vocational subject. Benefits to the Company are seen as increased confidence and communication leading to improved efficiency and responsiveness to training and change.

8.19 Local Learning and Skills Councils will be able to provide advice and practical help in setting up employee development schemes ensuring the maximum benefit to employers and employees. Working alongside this are individual learning accounts (see chapter 7) and the Government's new related tax relief measures for employers in support of employee development.

8.20 With the advent of much more flexible, on-line learning opportunities through the UfI, local Learning and Skills Councils will have an important role in helping businesses develop in-house learning centres and facilities. This work will be closely linked to the development of local sector networks and should maximise the opportunities for employers to work together and with providers in developing new programmes and shared resources.

8.21 Local Councils will also work with National Training Organisations and the Small Business Service to improve the quality of publicly funded in-company training. Beyond its role with publicly funded training the Small Business Service will have a wider advisory role. This might involve, for example, helping employers to be more intelligent purchasers of learning. This support would be part of a comprehensive package of services available through the Small Business Service.

8.22 These plans for delivery will be developed in conjunction with the Small Business Service. In delivering workforce development services and programmes, for example, the local Learning and Skills Council will arrange with the Small Business Service to provide a seamless service to small and medium sized businesses and to integrate skills development with enterprise and business competitiveness. This will include management development (including owner-management development), which is often the key to improving the performance of small firms. It will mean that Small Business Service staff will be the primary local point of contact with small firms for marketing of vocational training, Modern Apprenticeships, National Traineeships and Investors in People.

Question: Do you support our proposals for the role of the Learning and Skills Council at national and local level in relation to skills and workforce development?

CHAPTER 9

Transitional arrangements and timetable for implementing proposals

9.1 The changes we are planning will affect one way or another virtually every organisation involved in post-16 provision. We recognise that the next two years will be a challenging period for all involved in post-16 learning. Work will need to continue in order to achieve the ambitious targets we have set to increase participation, attainment and the quality of services we offer to young people and adults. Making the necessary changes in structures must not hinder that crucial task. At the same time, there must be an effective transition to the new arrangements.

The principles underpinning transition to the new arrangements

9.2 To achieve an effective transition we will:

- work closely with partners at national, regional and local level to draw up detailed plans for change;

- ensure that wherever possible expertise within the current system is utilised in the new arrangements. Many people working in the organisations affected will have an important role to play in the new arrangements;

- provide opportunities for people to update existing skills or acquire new ones to equip them for future roles;

- have clear and open communications;

- establish a new post-16 review implementation directorate within DfEE to work with other partners and help co-ordinate and manage the process of change.

9.3 We will look to partners at national, regional and local level to:

- continue to work closely together to drive up performance and meet the National Learning Targets;

- give Government early warning of emerging issues and work closely with us to resolve them;

- keep customers and the people who work for each organisation closely informed of progress.

The transition plan

9.4 Together with the DTI, DfEE is publishing at the same time as this White Paper the first draft of a transition plan which sets out:

- the aims for the transition period;

- the priciples which will underpin the transition;

- the steps which need to be taken over the next two years with time-bound milestones and a named 'owner' responsible for their progress.

9.5 We will use this first draft of the transition plan as a basis for detailed discussions with each organisation affected by our proposals. Our aim is to agree in due course with each its own detailed transition plan which will give clarity to both customers and the people working within those organisations about how the transition will be managed; and reassurance that it is being managed effectively. We will also update the national plan as key decisions are made over the coming months and share it with our partners. As well as working closely with individual organisations, we intend to establish an informal group involving key national partners as a sounding board to ensure that all the necessary linkages are being made.

9.6 During the transitional period, existing funding bodies will continue to have a duty to get best value for public money and to safeguard assets. We will work with these bodies, through our normal mechanisms, to ensure that this is the case. However, the Government reserves the right to take additional steps, including taking legislative powers where appropriate, to guarantee that our goals are met.

Headline timetable for the establishment of the Learning and Skills Council, the new inspection arrangements and the new advice and guidance service for young people

9.7 Set out below is a timetable for implementing the new arrangements. The timetable will be subject to the passage of the necessary legislation. More detailed timetables and arrangements for the transition period will be issued as part of the transition plan.

Month/ Year	Milestone
June 1999	DfEE publishes its plans and proposals in a White Paper
Summer 1999	Publish a consultation paper about the structure of the new support service for young people and the timetable for change
Autumn 1999	The White Paper consultation period ends
Autumn 1999	Regional Development Agencies (RDAs) propose boundaries of the local Learning and Skills Councils and Small Business Service areas
Autumn 1999	Decisions announced on the location of the national Learning and Skills Council and the boundaries of the local Learning and Skills Councils
Summer 2000	Appointment of Chair and Chief Executive of Learning and Skills Council
Summer 2000	Chairs and Executive Directors of local Learning and Skills Councils appointed
Summer - end 2000	Learning and Skills Council begins recruiting staff including identifying opportunities for people in existing organisations
Autumn 2000 - Spring 2001	Training of staff including, where necessary, updating skills
December 2000	The Secretary of State issues a Letter of Guidance (including amount of grant in aid) to the Learning and Skills Council
Early 2001 - Spring 2001	The Learning and Skills Council operates in parallel with existing bodies
April 2001	The Learning and Skills Council is fully operational

CHAPTER 10

Consultation - how to respond

We believe that these proposals will modernise and improve the current learning framework. At the same time, we recognise that the reforms we are planning will have an impact on all those who are involved in post-16 learning at national and local levels, including young and adult learners themselves. We want all those involved in, or affected by, post-16 learning to consider and discuss these proposals.

The main issues on which we have invited comment are:-

Chapter 3: The Learning and Skills Council

- What more might we do to ensure coherence between the work of the Learning and Skills Council and pre-16 learning?

- Are the proposed responsibilities of the local Learning and Skills Councils the right ones to ensure responsiveness at local level to the needs of local labour markets and communities?

- Are the functions described for the local Learning Partnerships the right ones to build on the momentum already generated?

- How can the local Learning Partnerships best work with and support the local Learning and Skills Councils?

- What more can we do to ensure accountability at local and national level?

Chapter 4: A framework for success beyond 16

- Is there more we should do to ensure that we strike the right balance between national arrangements and local flexibility and discretion?

- How can we ensure that the arrangements ensure integration of all the public funding available within the area?

- How can we ensure that the planning and funding arrangements support people with special needs?

- Are these the right set of critical success factors against which to evaluate the new arrangements?

- How can we ensure that the Learning and Skills Council and its local arms develop effective links with partners at national, regional and local level?

Chapter 5 - Improving quality

- What more should we do to ensure we drive up quality in post-16 provision?

Chapter 6 - Education and training of young people

- We will be announcing shortly the details of our new "Connexions" strategy and issuing a separate consultation document on our proposals for a new support service for young people.
- We are also publishing today a consultation paper on the funding of school sixth forms - see below.

Chapter 7 - Supporting adult learners

- In what further ways can the Learning and Skills Council best deliver improvements in adult learning?
- What more should we do to ensure we develop coherent provision for unemployed people to gain the skills they need and to tackle the other barriers they face in finding and keeping work?

Chapter 8 - Encouraging learning businesses

- Are the measures proposed sufficient to engage business in the new arrangements?
- Do you support our proposals for the role of the Learning and Skills Council at national and local level in relation to skills and workforce development?

Please let us have your comments by Friday 15 October 1999. You can respond:-

- **by post** to Mike Morley, Post-16 Review Implementation Group, Level 3, Department for Education and Employment, Moorfoot, Sheffield S1 4PQ
- **by email** to mike-morley.consultation@dfee.gov.uk

Responses may be made publicly available unless you state in your response that you wish it to remain confidential.

Braille, large print and audio cassette versions of the White Paper are available from Mike Morley at the above address.

Along with this White Paper (order reference P16LR), we are publishing:-

- a **summary version** (order reference P16LRS); and
- a consultation document, *'School Sixth Form Funding: a Consultation Paper'* (order reference P16LRCD).

Copies of these publications are available from:

DfEE Publications
Prolog,
PO Box 5050,
Sherwood Park,
Annesley,
Nottingham NG15 0DJ
Tel: 0845 602 2260
Fax: 0845 603 3360
Email: dfee@prologistics.co.uk.

A draft *'Transition Plan for Post-16 Education and Training and for Local Delivery of Support to Small Firms'* is also available. Copies of this document can be obtained from the Internet (see below for further information), or from:

Trevor Tucknutt,
TECSOP Division,
Level 3,
Department for Education and Employment,
Moorfoot,
Sheffield
S1 4PQ.

Internet access to this White Paper is now available, along with the documents listed above.
The internet address is: www.dfee.gov.uk/post16

Appendix 1

Implications for Scotland, Wales and Northern Ireland

Scotland
The education and training system in Scotland is very different from England, and direct comparisons are difficult. Scottish Enterprise and Highlands and Islands Enterprise contract with Local Enterprise Companies (LECs) who are responsible for the delivery of Government training programmes. *"Opportunities and Choices"*, a Consultation Paper on post-school provision for 16-18 year olds in Scotland was published in March 1999. It aims to stimulate ideas and encourage debate about the opportunities and choices which should be available in post-school provision. In February 1998 the Government accepted the Garrick Committee's recommendation that there should be two separate funding councils in Scotland, one for further education and one for higher education. The Scottish Further Education Funding Council (SFEFC) was established by Parliamentary Order on 1 January 1999.

Wales
The arrangements in Wales for the provision of post-16 education and training are currently similar to England's. Soon after the 1997 General Election, Welsh Office Ministers established the Education and Training Action Group for Wales (ETAG) which published its report *'An Education and Training Action Plan for Wales'* on 29th March. The plan will be submitted for consideration to the National Assembly of Wales, who will be responsible for taking decisions about the recommendations made by ETAG.

Northern Ireland
The education and training system in Northern Ireland is very different from England. The Training and Employment Agency is responsible for vocational training and delivers its programmes through contracts with providers. Further education is funded directly through the Department of Education Northern Ireland. Northern Ireland also has a unified Education and Training Inspectorate responsible for schools, further education and training programmes. Because of the very different arrangements in Northern Ireland there is very little read across to the changes being introduced for England. Northern Ireland Ministers have recently announced the outcome of an economic strategy review, Strategy 2010, following the earlier publication of proposals for taking forward Lifelong Learning in Northern Ireland. As a consequence of the Lifelong Learning proposals, a Northern Ireland Skills Task Force has been established and a consultation paper on the planning, funding and management of further and higher education has been published. These proposals build on the need to give employers a greater opportunity to influence post-16 provision; to improve cost effectiveness and value for money; and to raise the number of people engaged in learning.

Appendix 2

Information for monitoring and evaluation

Existing information on performance

1. DfEE and its partners already collect a wide range of statistical information that will be adapted and used to help measure success. This will be used to inform the plans produced by the new Council, including the setting of targets and reporting results based on relevant and consistent performance indicators for the sector as a whole.

2. We already have arrangements in place for monitoring progress towards the targets at national, regional and local levels using national information from surveys like the Labour Force Survey, the National Adult Learning Survey, and examination results data for schools and colleges. These sources and others like the new Learning and Training At Work Survey and the Youth Cohort Study will enable the measurement of progress on widening participation in education and training and in securing employer participation and contributions to the costs of learning. It will also be important to assess the impact of the new arrangements on those in particular ethnic groups; on people with disabilities; on those who face barriers to entering the labour market; and on those who seldom take part in learning.

National evaluation and review

3. It is important that evaluation focuses on the outcomes and impact of the new arrangements. We will also need to understand how the new arrangements are working and be able to identify areas for improvement and to disseminate good practice. To this end we will build on the systems for monitoring, research and evaluation which we and our partners already have in place such as the FEFC's Individual Student Record System and DfEE's Trainee Database System.

4. The new, integrated inspectorate regime will produce important information on the quality of provision. Inspection reports will be used by providers and the Learning and Skills Council. It will be essential for inspection findings to be taken into account by the local councils to inform their purchasing decisions. Inspection findings will also inform national reviews of quality.

Local evaluation

5. The new arrangements will give considerable discretion to the local Learning and Skills Councils in ensuring that provision meets needs at the grassroots. We will agree a framework with the national Learning and Skills Council within which the local plans shall be compiled, approved and outcomes monitored.

6. We will expect each local Learning and Skills Council to obtain good quality information about the local economy, community and labour market, and to agree a strategy for local development with the RDA and other partners. The plans of local Councils need to be designed taking full account of the local strategy; and local Councils will need to monitor and evaluate the impact of their activities in order continuously to improve their performance. We will work with the national Council to provide guidance and specify minimum core evaluation requirements, both to help local Councils and so that we can compile a comprehensive national picture of progress. Similar considerations will apply to other elements of the new arrangements, such as the new service to support young people.

Filling gaps in our knowledge

7. We will review our management information systems and requirements during the transition to the new arrangements to ensure that we have adequate information to compare the efficiency and effectiveness of the new and previous arrangements and to monitor progress. In particular we will, with our partners, design and implement an information system which:

- builds on the best features of the FEFC's Individual Student Record and DfEE's Trainee Database Systems;

- facilitates the tracking of individuals through the system;

- supports consistent and meaningful comparisons of performance (including retention and attainment), efficiency and effectiveness across different types of provision;

- provides relevant information at all levels of the system for:- students and potential students; providers; the national Council; local Learning and Skills Councils; and Government;

- supports the meaningful comparison of unit funding (e.g. per qualification) between different types of provision;

- supports the monitoring of the effect of training on the labour market experience of students; and

- enables an analysis of complaints and customer feedback.

8. Although a great deal of useful information will be drawn from existing and planned research and surveys, there are likely to be some important gaps which will become apparent as the detail of the new arrangements develops.

9. We will build on established procedures for the review, collection and use of statistical information and research, and will ensure that these are an integral part of the new Council's planning and prioritising arrangements. We will evaluate the individual components of the new arrangements with a view to ensuring that activities are properly co-ordinated. In all of this we will be seeking maximum benefit from the financial resources available, using cost benefit analysis and other techniques.

10. In measuring success, and identifying areas for improvement, we will also ensure commitment to mainstreaming equal opportunities. This will include systematic identification, assessment and action backed up with appropriate monitoring and evaluation as well as target setting, wherever appropriate, to address significant underachievement by women, men, people from different racial backgrounds, disabled people, or any minority or disadvantaged group.

Appendix 3

Current inspection and quality assurance arrangements

Post-16 quality assurance and inspection currently operate on a sectoral basis:

- the 1800 school sixth forms are inspected by OFSTED as part of a whole school inspection. OFSTED is a non-Ministerial Government Department set up by statute. It operates a 6-year inspection cycle. Wider support is provided by the duty on LEAs to improve school standards. Both have concentrated less on sixth forms than on other aspects of school provision;

- the 440 FE colleges are inspected by the Inspectorate arm of the FEFC. The Council is a statutory NDPB. The establishment of the Inspectorate derives from the duty placed on the FEFC to ensure that satisfactory arrangements exist to assess the quality of education in colleges within the sector. The Inspectorate operates a 4-year cycle. A Quality Improvement Unit has been established by the Council which is responsible for the administration of the Standards Fund. Wider support for colleges is provided by the Further Education Development Agency (FEDA);

- TEC-funded training by providers (and the education and training elements of the 18-24 New Deal options) is inspected by the Training Standards Council, which is a company limited by guarantee and a subsidiary of the TEC National Council. TECs themselves are responsible, through contract, for the quality of training delivered by their providers. The Council operates a 4-year cycle. Wider support is provided by development funds provided through DfEE;

- inspection of LEA arranged adult education services is the responsibility of OFSTED, as is the youth service. Given OFSTED's priorities for school inspection and, latterly, LEA inspections (which do not cover adult education at present) very little formal inspection work has been carried out in recent years. For 1999-2000 OFSTED have offered just 6 inspections, implying a 25 year cycle. Wider support should be provided by LEAs by quality assuring their own services by reference to OFSTED's inspection framework and criteria.

Bibliography

We found the following publications particularly helpful in writing this report:-

'A New Way of Learning: the UfI Network - Developing the University for Industry Concept', University for Industry, 1999

'Bargaining for Skills: Trade Unions and Training and Enterprise Councils Working in Partnership for Training', Trades Union Congress, 1995

'Bringing Britain Together: a National Strategy for Neighbourhood Renewal', Cm 4045, The Stationery Office, 1998

'Creating Learning Cultures: Next Steps in Achieving the Learning Age', DfEE, 1999

'Excellence in Cities', DfEE 1999

'Excellence in Schools', Cm 3681, The Stationery Office, 1997

'House of Commons Official Report' (Hansard), Wednesday 10 March 1999, vol 327, written answers, columns 214-215. Parliamentary written question from Mr Kidney to the Secretary of State for Education and Employment on the support given to Education Business Partnerships.

'Improving Literacy and Numeracy: a Fresh Start - the Report of the Working Group Chaired by Sir Claus Moser', DfEE, 1999

'Inclusive Learning: a Report of the Learning Difficulties and/or Disabilities Committee`, HMSO, 1996

'Individual Learning Accounts: a Summary of Progress', DfEE, 1999

'Learning for the Twenty-first Century: First Report of the National Advisory Group for Continuing Education and Lifelong Learning', National Advisory Group for Continuing Education and Lifelong Learning, DfEE, 1997

'Learning Works: Widening Participation in Further Education', FEFC, 1997

'Literacy Skills for the Knowledge Society', OECD, 1997

'National Adult Learning Survey 1997', DfEE, 1998

'National Learning Targets for England for 2002', DfEE, 1998

'National Survey of Careers Education and Guidance: Secondary Schools', OFSTED, 1998

'National Survey of Careers Education and Guidance: Special Schools and Pupil Referral Units', OFSTED, 1998

'Objective Setting and Monitoring in Executive Non Departmental Public Bodies', Cabinet Office, 1996

'Opening up Quangos: a Consultation Paper', Cabinet Office, 1997

'Opportunity Scotland: a Paper on Lifelong Learning', Cm 4048, The Stationery Office, 1998

'Qualifying for Success: a Consultation Paper on the Future of Post-16 Qualifications', DfEE, 1997

'Quinquennial Review of The Further Education Funding Council for England: Prior Options Review Report', DfEE, 1999

'Regional Development Agencies Act 1998', chapter 45, The Stationery Office, 1998

'Second Report of the National Skills Task Force: Delivering Skills for All', DfEE, 1999

'Standards in Public Life - Local Public Spending Bodies', Second Report of the Nolan Committee on Standards in Public Life, Cm 3270, The Stationery Office, 1996

'TECs: Meeting the Challenge of the Millennium - Consultation Paper', DfEE, 1998

'The Learning Age: a Renaissance for a New Britain', Cm 3790, The Stationery Office, 1998

'The Learning Age: Local Information, Advice and Guidance for Adults in England - Towards a National Framework', DfEE, 1998

'The Skills Audit: a Report from an Interdepartmental Group', DfEE/Cabinet Office, 1996

'Towards a National Skills Agenda: First Report of the National Skills Task Force', DfEE, 1998

Glossary

DfEE	Department for Education and Employment
DTI	Department of Trade and Industry
EBP	Education Business Partnership
ES	Employment Service
ESF	European Social Fund
FE	Further Education
FEDA	Further Education Development Agency
FEFC	Further Education Funding Council
GCE	General Certificate of Education
GCSE	General Certificate of Secondary Education
GNVQ	General National Vocational Qualification
GO	Government Office
HE	Higher Education
ICT	Information and Communication Technology
JSA	Jobseekers Allowance
LDA	London Development Agency
LEA	Local Education Authority
LSC	Learning and Skills Council
NACETT	National Advisory Council for Education and Training Targets
NDPB	Non Departmental Public Body
NEBP	National Education Business Partnership
NIACE	National Institute of Adult Continuing Education
NTO	National Training Organisation
NVQ	National Vocational Qualification
OFSTED	Office for Standards in Education
QCA	Qualifications and Curriculum Authority
RDA	Regional Development Agency
SBS	Small Business Service
SEU	Social Exclusion Unit
SME	Small and Medium-sized Enterprises
SRB	Single Regeneration Budget
TEC	Training and Enterprise Council
WEA	Workers Educational Association

Notes

Notes

Notes

Printed in the UK for the Stationery Office Limited
on behalf of the Controller of Her Majesty's Stationery Office
Dd 5068884 6/99 32956 Job No. J0084529